SpringerBriefs in Applied Sciences and Technology

SpringerBriefs present concise summaries of cutting-edge research and practical applications across a wide spectrum of fields. Featuring compact volumes of 50 to 125 pages, the series covers a range of content from professional to academic.

Typical publications can be:

- A timely report of state-of-the art methods
- An introduction to or a manual for the application of mathematical or computer techniques
- A bridge between new research results, as published in journal articles
- A snapshot of a hot or emerging topic
- An in-depth case study
- A presentation of core concepts that students must understand in order to make independent contributions

SpringerBriefs are characterized by fast, global electronic dissemination, standard publishing contracts, standardized manuscript preparation and formatting guidelines, and expedited production schedules.

On the one hand, **SpringerBriefs in Applied Sciences and Technology** are devoted to the publication of fundamentals and applications within the different classical engineering disciplines as well as in interdisciplinary fields that recently emerged between these areas. On the other hand, as the boundary separating fundamental research and applied technology is more and more dissolving, this series is particularly open to trans-disciplinary topics between fundamental science and engineering.

Indexed by EI-Compendex, SCOPUS and Springerlink.

More information about this series at http://www.springer.com/series/8884

Enrico Cicalò

Graphic Intelligence

Drawing and Cognition

 Springer

Enrico Cicalò
Dipartimento di Architettura,
Design e Urbanistica
University of Sassari
Alghero, Italy

ISSN 2191-530X   ISSN 2191-5318   (electronic)
SpringerBriefs in Applied Sciences and Technology
ISBN 978-3-030-45243-8   ISBN 978-3-030-45244-5   (eBook)
https://doi.org/10.1007/978-3-030-45244-5

This Springer imprint is published by the registered company Springer Nature Switzerland AG
The registered company address is: Gewerbestrasse 11, 6330 Cham, Switzerland

Preface

Starting from the discussion on the theory of multiple intelligences discussed by Howard Gardner in his famous work *Frame's of Mind*, this book presents and discusses the hypothesis of a particular form of intelligence, which will be named as *graphic intelligence*. This expression identifies the ability to use graphic abilities and, more generally, the ability to integrate the use of eye, mind and hand to solve problems of various kinds and generate effective products aimed at the creation, acquisition and communication of knowledge.

The most recent studies in the field of cognitive sciences suggest the existence of important relationships between graphic representation and cognitive development that support the idea of a graphic intelligence detectable among the other forms of intelligence capable of describing and containing a range of human intellectual competences.

As well as verbal languages, also drawing can be legitimately defined as a medium because it is not only a graphic translation of thought, but is itself a form of thought, besides being a product of thought. Thus, *graphic intelligence* would be confronted equally with the best-known linguistic and logical-mathematical intelligences on which the school and the curricula today tend to focus more and to complete and enrich the already investigated visual and spatial intelligences that, according to the literature produced so far on the subject, include and coordinate with the graphic skills.

Generally, stimuli related to graphic representation and communication gradually decay as the child grows, peaking in the early years of kindergarten and then slowly fading away at the end of secondary school. The observation of the process of activation, learning and evolution of the graphic sign starting from kindergarten, and the analysis of teaching methods and tools, allow to evaluate the contribution of graphic thought, expression, communication and visual perception in the development of design and creative skills, as well as imaginative and perceptive abilities.

Can graphic and visual education really contribute to the evolutive development, growth and formation of the individual? Is it by chance that the difficulties in the graphic and visual field are consistent with a more general impoverishment of the linguistic, expressive and imaginative abilities of most of the young adults facing university courses? What role does the ability to express oneself graphically play in individual cognitive development? Can this ability increase cognitive potential? How do these skills develop and how can they be stimulated within educational paths? These are the questions that this volume tries to answer, investigate or at least suggest ideas for future studies.

Each research starts from the observation of particular clues that are resonant in the mind and stimulate the curiosity of the scholars, orienting them to the development of a research path. In this case, there are two different inputs from which the investigation presented in this book started. The first is related to the observation of the spontaneity with which children use graphic languages in early childhood; the second, by contrast, concerns the observation of the loss of this spontaneity and the almost total lack of use of graphic languages in young adults. The contrast between these two phenomena reveals the vertical fall of the ability to draw that Richard Sennett defines as the divorce between hand and head.

A book that talks about images cannot but speak through images, and if it wants to discuss the value of their production as an instrument of thought it needs their use. For this reason, in parallel with the texts will be used complementary and never didactic images. The graphic language, in fact, as we will discuss in this work, is able to translate thought into that 'cursive' form which allows us to capture the rapid flow of mental images that are processed in our heads. The images presented in this volume have been chosen not only because they are illustrative and significant of what has been discussed, but also because they demonstrate clearly how drawing can enhance cognitive processes and knowledge building.

The choice of the iconographic apparatus—fundamental in the development of this research—was facilitated by the wide availability of images accessible on the web and, above all, by the possibility of consulting the digitized archives made accessible by the most important public and private institutions; just think, for example, of the archive of Isaac Newton's writings published by the University of Cambridge Digital Library, The Thomas Edison Papers Project of the Rutgers University, or Fellini's drawings that can be consulted in the archives of the Federico Fellini Foundation. Also thanks to the consultation of these sources, the book tries to make available to the reader a relevant and illustrative iconographic repertory on graphic intelligence in its different forms and applied to the different possible fields of investigation. The availability of these sources opens a further possible field of research for the study of the relations between thought processing and graphic representation.

The study here presented adopts Howard Gardner's theory on multiple intelligence as a starting point in the discussion of different forms of intelligence in order to better analyze and understand a particular area of human intellectual capacity that is that of drawing and graphic representation. According to the theory of multiple intelligences, discussed in Chap. 1, human intellectual competences are many, relatively autonomous and their nature and number is not exactly definable, also because different intellectual capacities tend to shape and combine in a variety of adaptive ways. For this reason, Gardner's theory takes into consideration the possibility of candidating certain abilities to be defined as a particular form of intelligence through the satisfaction of certain requirements.

The analysis discussed in this volume also focuses on the use of the words 'spatial', 'visual' and 'graphic', which often assume different meanings in the various disciplines and theories, but always remain strongly connected in relationships of interdependence or subordination depending on the authors and disciplinary views. Therefore, we try to investigate the different meanings of these words in relation to the forms of intelligence connected to them in order to hypothesize the possibility of isolating a particular form of intelligence, the graphic intelligence.

Following the analysis of the different meanings of the terms 'visual' and 'graphic', in Chap. 2, it is investigated then the concept of graphic skills and graphic communication, considered as different from the more investigated 'visual communication' in order to emphasize the aspects related to the coding of the message rather than those related to decoding on which studies on visual communication are more oriented. The processes of visual perception and graphic representation, although strongly connected, are different mechanisms whose understanding is fundamental to understand graphic intelligence and graphic skills. So we compare these two aspects starting from the functioning of the cognitive processes on which perception and representation are based, going so far as to affirm that visual perception and graphic representation can be considered two sides of the same coin: if visual perception can be seen as a process of decoding the visual stimuli that the mind receives, graphic representation can instead be considered as a process of coding the signs that must then be perceived and decoded by the eye.

In Howard Gardner's discussion of multiple intelligences, spatial intelligence would embrace both the sphere of visual and graphic skills, however, highlighting important differences. The adjectives 'spatial' and 'visual' would, from his point of view, be usable as synonyms since all spatial competences can only arise from vision. Graphic skills would also be part of the large family of spatial skills but they would still lend themselves to be analyzed in an autonomous way, allowing you to hypothesize and then verify the graphic intelligence, making it possible to hypothesize and then verify the graphic intelligence, as discussed in Chap. 3.

Once discussed the relationships between graphic intelligence and scientific investigation (Chap. 4), and after having used them to demonstrate the autonomy and the role of this kind of intelligence in the development of scientific thought and in the evolution of the history of science, the role of graphic intelligence is explored in relation to the professional and educational fields in which it is most exercised so as to highlight which cognitive processes it will be able to activate. The relations between graphic intelligence and design action can be considered the highest example of the use of graphic intelligence for thought development. During their training and experience, designers acquire a modus operandi that makes graphic language and graphic thought the privileged tool for the production of ideas and for the representation of the projects on which their professional activity revolves (Chap. 5). The ability to use it in parallel and at the same time alternatively to verbal language, the ability to translate mental images into drawings, makes their graphic ability a model that should be taken as a reference not only in specialist training but also in generalist training.

In the awareness that each of the paragraphs of this chapter would require to be explored more deeply, other fields of investigation such as sciences, arts, literature, cinema and theatre are equally significant and illustrative of how graphic intelligence can be a fundamental tool in the most diverse professional fields (Chap. 6).

Graphic intelligence can not only be an effective tool for enhancing thinking and producing knowledge but can also be a powerful learning tool. Starting from the learning by doing approach and from the traditional use of images as a learning strengthening tool, in Chap. 7 is discussed the role of drawing in memorizing information and in learning processes.

Science, design, art as well as learning processes cannot benefit from the advantages of such intellectual abilities unless they are adequately stimulated. For this reason, in Chap. 8 is discussed the role of graphic intelligence in training and learning from childhood to adulthood.

Finally, in Chap. 9, some concluding notes indicate possible ways to strengthen graphic intelligence and recover the cognitive potential linked to it, to which our entire culture and history are indebted.

Alghero, Italy   Enrico Cicalò

Contents

Chapter 1
Multiple Intelligences

1.1 The Theory of Multiple Intelligences

In the book *Frames of Mind. The Theory of Multiple Intelligence* (1983), Howard Gardner—Professor of Cognitive Sciences at Harvard University—defines intelligence as the ability to solve problems or create valued products within a cultural context. When talking about intelligence, Gardner does not attribute a particular positive quality to the word *intelligence*, even though in our culture it has a decidedly positive connotation. His idea of intelligence is rather closer to the concept of 'potential' than to that of 'talent'.

Gardner's studies start from a critique of how intelligence is measured through standardized tests aimed at assessing scholastic potential that focuses on linguistic and logical-mathematical skills and is therefore unable to fully evaluate different individual skills. In order to adequately understand the field of human cognition, Howard Gardner includes and considers a much broader and more universal set of skills and competences than those usually considered in traditional educational curricula.

From this point of view, the forms of intelligence would be multiple and relatively independent of each other. While recognizing the concatenation between different forms of intelligence in all complex human activities, Gardner argues that the isolation of different intelligences can be the right way to a better understanding of human cognition. The debate within the cognitive sciences on these issues has then developed further, but its discussion is not the aim of this volume in which Gardner's theory will be rather adopted as a starting point in the discussion of the different forms of intelligence in order to better analyze and understand a particular area of human intellectual capacity: that of graphic representation.

Before Gardner, several authors studied the different forms of intelligence. Thorndike (1920), Thorndike et al. (1926) conceived intelligence as the sum of three parts: abstract intelligence, mechanical intelligence and social intelligence. Thurstone (1938, 1941) argued that intelligence consists of seven primary abilities. Guilford (1957), Guilford and Hoepfner (1971) analyzed intelligence as consisting of

© The Author(s), under exclusive license to Springer Nature Switzerland AG 2020
E. Cicalò, *Graphic Intelligence*, SpringerBriefs in Applied Sciences
and Technology, https://doi.org/10.1007/978-3-030-45244-5_1

four content categories, five operational categories, six product categories, proposing 150 different intellectual faculties. Sternberg (1986, 1989) proposed a triarchic theory of intelligence that identified analytic, creative and practical intelligence. Finally, Ceci (1990) has explored the multiple cognitive potentials that allow for knowledge to be acquired.

The theory of multiple intelligences states that human intellectual competences are several, relatively autonomous from each other and their nature and their number is difficult to define, also because the different intellectual abilities tend to be shaped and combined with each other in a variety of adaptive ways. For this reason, this theory suggests the possibility of proposing certain abilities for being defined and studied as a specific form of intelligence, if they meet the requirements that Gardner makes available to those who wish to try to isolate a particular form of intelligence. These are the criteria for the identification of intelligence:

- if the abilities connected to this form of intelligence can be separately destroyed or preserved in the presence of brain damage;
- if there are individuals who exceptionally develop that skill, also despite a delay in the development of other skills:
- if it has a distinct neural representation, that is, its neural structure and functioning are distinguishable from that of other major human faculties;
- if it has a distinct developmental history, that is, different intelligences should develop at different rates and along paths that are distinctive;
- if it is possible to locate its evolutionary antecedents;
- if it is possible to materialize it in a symbolic system;
- if it is supported by evidence from psychometric tests of intelligence;
- if it is distinguishable from other intelligences through experimental psychological tasks.

However, the exploration of a possible form of intelligence, the graphic one, that this volume proposes, is not based, on a discussion of the compliance with the requirements indicated by Gardner. As he himself specifies, these forms of intelligence are actually only fictions; useful fictions, however, that allows us to discuss processes and abilities that actually form a continuum, like all things in nature. The isolation of individual forms of intelligence is indicated as a useful possibility to enlighten scientific problems and to face practical problems. The individual forms of intelligence are therefore potentially valid scientific constructs on which Gardner bases his treatment of the different intellectual competences that he structures into seven main families of intelligence: linguistic, musical, logical-mathematical, spatial, bodily-kinaesthetic, intrapersonal interpersonal. After some years Howards added further forms of intelligence as the naturalist intelligence, the existential intelligence and the pedagogical intelligence.

The two most important scientific implications of the theory of multiple intelligences are complementary. On the one hand, all human beings possess these intelligences. On the other hand, no two human beings—not even identical twins—exhibit precisely the same profile of intelligences. That is because even when genetics are controlled for (as is the case with monozygotic twins), individuals have different life experiences and are also motivated to differentiate themselves from one another.

Following are listed and described the intelligences analyzed by Howard:

- Linguistic Intelligence: An ability to analyze information and create products involving oral and written language such as speeches, books and memos;
- Logical-Mathematical Intelligence: the ability to develop equations and proofs, make calculations and solve abstract problems;
- Spatial Intelligence: the ability to recognize and manipulate large-scale and fine-grained spatial images;
- Musical Intelligence: the ability to produce, remember and make meaning of different patterns of sound;
- Bodily-Kinaesthetic Intelligence: the ability to use one's own body to create products or solve problems;
- Interpersonal Intelligence: the ability to recognize and understand other people's moods, desires, motivations and intentions;
- Intrapersonal Intelligence: the ability to recognize and understand his or her own moods, desires, motivations and intentions;
- Naturalist Intelligence: the ability to identify and distinguish among different types of plants, animals and weather formations that are found in the natural world;
- Existential intelligence: the ability that leads human beings to pose big 'existential questions';
- Pedagogical intelligence: the intelligence that enables human beings to convey knowledge and skills to other human beings who have varying degrees of knowledge.

1.1.1 Spatial, Visual and Graphic

In Howard Gardner's discussion of multiple intelligences, existing intelligences are more deeply investigated in their several sub-intelligences. Thus, spatial intelligence would embrace both the sphere of visual and graphic skills, although it would highlight important differences. From his point of view, the adjectives 'spatial' and 'visual' could be used as synonyms because all spatial competences can only be born from vision. Graphic skills would also be part of the large family of spatial skills but, as we will see in the next chapters, they would still lend themselves to being analyzed independently.

Furthermore, although the concepts 'spatial' and 'visual' are often used as synonyms, Gardner argues that it might be more appropriate to propose the adjective 'visual' instead of 'spatial' because, in humans, the spatial intelligence is closely related to their observation of the visual world and develops from it in the most direct way. However, the perception of an object or a form does not necessarily occur through sight, so this visual connotation of perception can be limiting. Gardner writes that as linguistic intelligence is not entirely dependent on the vocal-auditive channels and can also develop in an individual lacking these means of communication, so also spatial intelligence can develop even in an individual who is blind and therefore does not have direct access to the visual world. Therefore, it seems better to speak of spatial intelligence without inseparably connecting it with any particular sensory mode.

The terms 'spatial', 'visual' and 'graphic' often assume different meanings in the various disciplines and theories, but always remain strongly interconnected in relationships sometimes of interdependence and sometimes of subordination depending on the authors and disciplinary views. In the context of literature on the sciences of graphic representation, we discover that the dimension of the three spheres—'spatial', 'visual' and 'graphic'—is defined differently. Gary Bertoline considers visual science as the science that contains both the spatial and the graphic spheres (Bertoline 1998), always looking at graphic communication as part of visual science (Bertoline and Wiebe 1997).

1.2   Spatial Intelligence and Its Possible Sub-intelligences

1.2.1   Spatial Intelligence

Spatial intelligence was included by L. L. Thurstone in 1938 among the 'seven primary facts of the intellect' (Verbal Understanding, Verbal Fluidity, Numerical Capacity, Spatial Visualization, Memory, Reasoning, Perceptual Speed), then in 1983 by H. Gardner among the 'seven forms of intelligence' (linguistic, musical, logical-mathematical, spatial, corporeal-kinaesthetic, intrapersonal, interpersonal) as well as other theories have always focused attention on the visual-spatial sphere.

Within Howard Gardner's theory of multiple intelligences, intelligence is defined as a particular form of human intellectual competence that involves a set of problem-solving skills that allows the individual to solve difficulties also through the creation of an effective product; moreover, it must itself involve the ability to find a solution to problems, thus preparing the ground for the acquisition of new knowledge.

Many problems can be addressed through linguistic or mathematical propositions, others, especially in the field of objects and images, cannot be solved through these languages and need to be set as problems of visual imagination. This capacity is traditionally separated from the logical and linguistic ones and is often defined as 'the other intelligence'; it is that spatial intelligence based on non-verbal languages opposed to and at the same time complementary to the intelligences based on linguistic propositions.

Spatial intelligence has been defined by Howard Gardner as the composition of different interconnected abilities that operate as a family and are capable of strengthening each other, such as the ability to recognize examples of the same element;

the ability to transform the same element into another or to recognize such transformation; the ability to produce a graphical representation of spatial information. Therefore, according to Gardner, graphic skills are part of spatial intelligence, which would also be the basis of the ability to represent the real world two-dimensionally or three-dimensionally through symbolic codifications, as in the case of maps, diagrams or geometric figures. The sensitivity to the various lines of force that enter a representation is also traced back to spatial intelligence, where lines of force are defined as the perception of those elements that contribute to the effectiveness of the representation such as tension, balance and composition that characterize a painting, a sculpture as well as many natural elements.

In the literature, however, it is possible to find some different approaches that attempt to isolate the individual aspects of spatial intelligence. They are, for example, visual intelligence, perceptual intelligence and design intelligence. Some clues open the way towards the exploration of graphic intelligence, passing through the visual, perceptive and design ones that will be briefly explained in the following paragraphs.

1.2.2   Perceptive Intelligence

As said, according to this approach, the ability to perceive, visualize and represent would be closely linked and potentially referable to a single form of intelligence. Spatial intelligence can be considered closely related to the observation of the visual world and develops from it in the most direct way. The ability to perceive the world with precision, to execute transformations and modifications of one's initial perceptions and to succeed in recreating aspects of one's visual experience even in the absence of relevant stimuli are often considered among the most characteristic aspects of spatial intelligence.

Appiano (1998), on the other hand, isolates the concept of perceptive intelligence to define the ability to capture and preserve every stimulus coming from both external reality and the internal world, from culture as well as from emotions. Appiano considers the visual perception of external reality and visualization through the 'eye of the mind' as two expressions of the same form of intelligence. However, the ability to process mental images and visualize with the 'eye of the mind' (Ferguson 1978) is not necessarily linked to perceptual abilities. In fact, the existence of a perceptual system common to both tactile and visual modes have been demonstrated, whereby the mental images that individuals generally form through visual perception can actually be accessible to the blind on the basis of tactile experiences (Kennedy 1974). The ability to perceive through sight and to visualize mental images can, therefore, be analyzed separately through the two autonomous concepts of perceptive intelligence and visual intelligence.

1.2.3 Visual Intelligence

Even Damasio (1999) argues that the two processes of perception and visualization, even though they are connected, can be isolated. The brain has been selected by natural evolution to know the external environment on the basis of the changes it undergoes as a result of interactions with objects and the processes of reality with which it comes into contact and interacts. Based on this physical interaction with the environment, the brain thinks and acts through images. The use of images is, in fact, the most effective way for the brains of mammals to rapidly pass information through various brain interfaces.

Furthermore, Ann Marie Barry, in her book *Visual Intelligence: Perception, Image and the Manipulation of the Visual in Communications* (1997), argues that perception is the basis of knowledge and understanding, and that visual intelligence is necessary not only to resist the influence of passively absorbed messages but also to develop the ability to think in an abstract and perceptually oriented way. According to Barry, the concept of visual intelligence suggests new perceptual potentials and expands communication and cognitive possibilities. Perception is not, according to this approach, a simple recording of the external world but a mental process by which we interpret reality as an image.

1.2.4 Design Intelligence

Design thinking differs from abstract visual thinking precisely because of its need to be translated through various types of models, physical or graphic (Cross 1986). Design intelligence also benefits from a wide family of different skills, including visual and graphic skills, and more generally requires the ability to use non-verbal forms of communication (Cross 1982). Although design intelligence is not explicitly part of the large family of visual-spatial skills, its discussion and exploration of literature on the subject allow the introduction of graphic intelligence, on which the design action is based. In analyzing design intelligence, Anita Cross (1986) states that it depends heavily on graphic skills and recognizes their fundamental role in the production of ideas. As discussed in the cognitive models studied bySommers (1984), drawing implies the definition of adequate strategies to solve a problem of representation. When the subject to be represented is not known and there are no known and consolidated routine strategies available, the designer activates his own graphic intelligence to define optimal methods to solve the complex problems given (Cross 1986).

1.2.5 Graphic Intelligence

Gardner (1983) brings together different skills within the same family and specifies that they are different skills. An individual, for example, can have an acute visual perception, while having little ability to draw, imagine or transform an absent world. Although it is difficult to develop graphic skills without the support of adequate visual and perceptual skills, one can see without necessarily being able to translate one's own perception graphically.

Referring to Piaget's studies (Piaget and Inhelder 1948) on the development of children's spatial understanding, Gardner points out that children from the age of three are able to orient themselves in space and select and recognize landmarks in the landscape, but the representation of this knowledge poses a series of difficulties. Even older children find it hard to express their intuitive knowledge of a place's plan in some other form. Thus, a five or six-year-old child can orient himself satisfactorily in a place, even if unfamiliar; however, if asked to describe it in words, or to draw a drawing or a map of it, he will either fail at all or provide an essentially oversimplified and therefore useless explanation (describing the path as a straight line, for example, even if in reality it is very complex). The most difficult task for school children is to coordinate their knowledge in a map of a place, achieved through various different experiences, in a single organized reference system. To express themselves in different terms, children are now able to orient themselves in many places in their neighbourhood or in their city, and in fact, they never find what they are looking for. However, they often lack the ability to draw a map, an approximate scheme or to provide a general verbal explanation of the relationship between places. The representation of their fragmentary knowledge in another form or in a system of symbols reveals itself to be an elusive part of spatial intelligence. Perhaps we could say: while children's spatial understanding develops rapidly, the expression of this understanding through another intelligence or through a symbolic code remains difficult (Gardner 1983).

Therefore, in referring to another form of intelligence responsible for the graphic expression of spatial concepts, Gardner seems to open the way for the definition and the deepening of that graphic intelligence that will be investigated in the next chapters.

References

A. Appiano, *Manuale di immagine: intelligenza percettiva, creatività progetto.* (Meltemi, 1998)

A.M.S. Barry, *Visual Intelligence: Perception, Image, and Manipulation in Visual Communication* (State University of New York Press, Albany, NY, 1997)

G.R. Bertoline, Visual science: an emerging discipline. J. Geom. Graph. (1998)

G.R. Bertoline, E.N. Wiebe, Fundamentals of Graphics Communication. Chicago: Irwin Graphics Series. Trad. it. 2003. Fondamenti di comunicazione grafica (McGraw-Hill, Milano, 1997), pp. 651

S.J. Ceci, *On Intelligence–more or Less: A Bio-ecological Treatise on Intellectual Development.*
(Prentice Hall, Upper Saddle River, NJ, 1990)

N. Cross, Designerly way of knowing. Des. Stud. **3**(4) (1982)

A. Cross, Design intelligence: the use of codes and language systems in design. Des. Stud. (1986)

A.R. Damasio, *The Feeling of What Happens: Body and Emotion in the Making of Consciousness*
(Harcourt Brace & Company, New York, 1999)

E.S. Ferguson, The mind's eye: nonverbal thought in technology. Science (1978)

H. Gardner, *Frames of Mind: The Theory of Multiple Intelligence* (Basic Books, New York, NY,
USA, 1983)

J.P. Guilford, *The Nature of Human Intelligence* (McGraw-Hill, New York, 1957)

J.P. Guilford, R. Hoepfner, *The Analysis of Intelligence.* (McGraw-Hill, New York, 1971)

J.M. Kennedy, *A Psychology of Picture Perception: Images and Information* (Jossey Bass, San
Francisco, 1974). H. Gardner, *Frames of Mind: The Theory of Multiple Intelligence* (Basic Books,
New York, 1983)

J. Piaget, B. Inhelder, *La, représentation de l'espace chez l'enfant* (Presses Universitaires de France,
Paris, 1948)

R.J. Sternberg, *Intelligence Applied: Understanding and Increasing Your Intellectual Skills*
(Harcourt Brace, San Diego, 1986)

R.J. Sternberg, *The Triarchic Mind: A new Theory of Human Intelligence* (Penguin Books, New
York, 1989)

E.L. Thorndike, Intelligence examinations for college entrance. J. Educ. Res. **1**(5), 329–337 (1920)

E.L. Thorndike, E.O. Bregman, M.V. Cobb, E. Woodyard, Measur. Intell. (1926)

L.L. Thurstone, Primary mental abilities. Psychometric Monogr. (1), (1938). H. Gardner, *Frames
of Mind. The Theory of Multiple Intelligence* (Basic Books, New York, 1983)

P. Van Sommers, *Drawing and Cognition: Descriptive and Experimental Studies of Graphic
Production Processes* (Cambridge University Press, New York, NY, USA, 1984)

Chapter 2
Graphic Skills

In discussing the different forms of intelligence, the different meanings of the terms 'visual' and 'graphic' have so far been highlighted. In the light of these different meanings, this chapter is dedicated to the exploration of graphic skills with the aim of emphasizing more the aspects related to the coding of the message rather than those related to decoding, on which studies on 'visual communication' are more oriented. Although the processes of visual perception and graphic representation are strongly connected to each other, they are autonomous processes whose understanding is fundamental for comprehending graphic intelligence and graphic skills. In this chapter, the two processes are discussed and compared starting from the functioning of the cognitive processes on which perception and representation are based. Visual perception and graphic representation can be considered two sides of the same coin. If visual perception can, in fact, be seen as the process of decoding the visual stimuli that the mind receives, graphic representation can instead be considered the process of coding the signs that must then be perceived and decoded by the eye.

In this way, the gaze performs a back and forth journey in the territory of communication thanks to which in one sense the signs of the graphic representation are codified and in the opposite sense they are decoded through visual perception. The path that connects visual perception and graphic representation is the one that daily and continuously undertakes the looks and minds of anyone who has to deal with a message whose transmission has been entrusted to a graphic language.

2.1 Graphic Languages

The language of images is one of the most powerful tools available to man to shape reality. It can be given a fundamental ethical and social role, as Kepes (1986) acknowledges. Kepes claims that the language of vision, visual communication is capable of spreading knowledge more effectively than almost any other means of communication. It allows man to express and report his experiences in an objective form.

© The Author(s), under exclusive license to Springer Nature Switzerland AG 2020
E. Cicalò, *Graphic Intelligence*, SpringerBriefs in Applied Sciences
and Technology, https://doi.org/10.1007/978-3-030-45244-5_2

Visual communication is universal and international: it has no limitations imposed by language, vocabulary or grammar and can be understood by both the illiterate and the educated person; it can convey facts and ideas to a wider and deeper extent than any other means of communication (Kepes 1986).

Today, in particular, individuals located in all parts of the world gather with their baggage of languages and experiences around the new technological tools of communication contributing to the construction of a new contemporary Babel from which the eternal need to find common and shared platforms able to allow exchanges and allow communication re-emerges. There are three possible ways in which over time we have tried to respond to this need.

The first is to translate the message with the words of all the possible or probable languages that can be known by the interlocutors; this solution is difficult to implement because it is particularly complex and costly. As it is difficult to translate the message into all possible languages, the specular solution that would provide that all users could share a single language chosen as universal is equally ineffective.

This is the second possible strategy that foresees entrusting the message to a language known to all, or at least to most. This last path has been investigated over time through various attempts that have seen alternating both the construction of new idioms and the alternation of different languages elected to universal according to the influence and predominance of different nations and cultures.

In global and globalized communication, the use of national idioms is limited by the need to make specific language codes shared between issuer and receiver. The search for some form of universal communication often ends up giving confidence to another language that does not require the learning of codes belonging to cultures and populations but whose codes are connected to the very nature of human beings. They are the codes of those languages that replace images with words, entrusting the communication of the most complex messages to one of the most spontaneous, rapid and natural mechanisms of reading and interpreting reality: visual perception.

In an era dominated by the widespread diffusion of communication tools that allow people to be connected to their geographical location or to their linguistic or cultural identity, visual messages gain a renewed centrality thanks to their ability to match the speed of the most up-to-date communication tools and to contribute to overcoming possible linguistic and cultural barriers. With the advent of new technologies and new modes of communication, as well as with the emergence of an increasingly globalized economy, the characteristics of graphic languages, with their speed and universality, seem to be among the most appropriate to respond to the new demands of communication. This is what is happening in the most varied fields of communication, from the emoticons of the most up-to-date social networks to the assembly instructions for furniture put on the market by companies that are becoming more and more successful on a global level; from road signs and environmental graphics for orientation in public spaces to the confirmation of the validity of the most classic and timeless forms of graphic transmission of knowledge and information, such as scientific representations and technical works in the most varied disciplines, which end up entrusting the diffusion of their contents to graphic languages as they are able to represent synthetically the most varied types and levels of complexity.

An ordinary object that traces a mark on any surface; the prehistoric man who carves the rock with a harder stone; the boy who traces marks on the asphalt with chalk; the prisoner who reconstructs a world of marks on the wall-diaphragm that separates him from the outside world; Archimedes who draws figures on the sand and who lets himself be killed so as not to interrupt the dialogue with those shapes (legend: but the legend means); the hundreds of draftsmen who go through the work-shops of France to trace the tables of the Encyclopedia; the researchers of almost all disciplines who, having reached certain limits in their knowledge that can be expressed with the word, find with a non-verbal sign the possibility to go further (Massironi 1989). Massironi wrote this list of subjects who have used graphic skills and graphic notation, simple signs visible on a surface, to describe or explain a world of phenomena; and it could continue for a long time to come. Graphic language is an instrument so simple, but also so intrinsically flexible as to allow the narration of the most diverse ways of the complexity and increasingly expandable to cover expressive possibilities (Massironi 1989). Although the language of images cannot be considered a perfect language (Eco 1993), images do not require knowledge of the many, complex and always different lexical and grammatical structures that characterize verbal communication, but require only the ability to visually perceive the inputs from the reality observed by the user, a capacity rooted in the very nature of man and developed during his evolution, for questions of survival rather than aesthetic enjoyment, and therefore available to all.

2.2 Graphic Communication

The language of vision, through images, is able to transmit a message more effectively than any other means of communication. Although there are limits linked to the socio-cultural context in which the message is transmitted and received, visual communication is considered universal. Since it is less limited by the need to know and govern complex grammatical, orthographic, lexical and syntactical codes, graphic language can be understood by both the illiterate and the educated person, favouring the transmission of facts, ideas and information more effectively than any other means of communication.

In the classic scheme of how communication works, the transmitting subject is the one who puts the graphic signs into code so that they can be decoded by the observer, i.e. the final receiver of the visual message transmitted. The channel in which this communication takes place, i.e. the medium through which the broadcaster conveys and through which the receiver obtains the message, is visual. Visual communication takes place through the use of graphic languages encoded through the techniques of graphic representation and decoded through the processes of visual perception that are spontaneously triggered whenever an individual finds himself observing an image.

Visual perception and graphic representation can, therefore, be considered two sides of the same coin. The gaze makes a return trip in the territory of visual communication thanks to which in one sense the signs of the graphic representation are codified and in the opposite sense, they are decoded through visual perception. It is that journey that links visual perception and graphic representation, visual skills and graphic skills and that daily and continuously engages the eyes and minds of anyone who is confronted with a message whose transmission is entrusted to visual communication. Perception can, in fact, be assimilated to a process of 'decoding' reality external to the observer; it involves attribution of meaning and an acquisition of meaning. Graphic representation, on the other hand, can be seen as a 'coding', i.e. as a process through which graphic signs are chosen, constructed and juxtaposed in order to transmit a certain meaning (Massironi 1989). Knowing the mechanisms of visual perception, the strategies of the glance allows to strategically design the graphic representation in order to consciously guide the perception and make the visual communication effective.

2.3 Visual Perception—Graphic Representation

Of the five senses, sight is generally considered the most important. Perception, communication and human participation in the outside world derive to a large extent from the mediating role played by the visual organ. Visual perception is the result of a series of complex actions through which we can see. Sense devoted to the understanding of the surrounding reality, sight in the course of man's evolution has refined its mechanisms of functioning in relation to the perception of risk situations and survival itself, even before the mere aesthetic enjoyment closer to the traditional contemporary conception.

However, vision, that is the process of perception of images, does not depend solely on the eyes. It arises from the integrated action between eye and brain from which the psychic, mental images originate. We, therefore, observe reality with the brain as well as with the eye. Reality is perceived by the eyes which, through the optic nerve, transmit photochemical and bioelectric signals in the visual area of the cerebral cortex, which in turn elaborates its own reality, which is what we perceive. At the origin of the perceptive process, there is the light that passes through the eye and is transformed into nerve impulses, which, processed by the cerebral cortex, are translated into sensations.

The production of sensations through visual perception has been explored by the theory of form, or Gestalt Theorie, according to which visual stimuli are organized and processed by our brain fields in relation to external stimuli producing sensations. The participation of the mind makes perception an experience that is not static and objective but creative, dynamic and subjective. Perceiving an image implies the participation of the observer in an organizational and interpretative process that leads to the shaping of sensory impressions into a unified and organic whole, producing a plastic experience (Kanisza 1980).

2.3.1 *Visual Decoding*

The process by which we visually perceive reality and decode visual stimuli was studied by Kandel (2012) who divided it into three stages. The first stage, which begins in the retina, is low-level visual processing. This stage establishes the characteristics of a particular visual scene by identifying the position of an object in space and identifying its colour. The second stage, starting in the primary cortex, is the intermediate-level visual processing. It assembles simple linear segments, each with a specific orientation axis, obtaining contours that define the boundaries of an image, and builds a unified perception of the shape of an object. This process is called contour integration. At the same time, the intermediate-level of vision separates the object from the background in a process called surface segmentation. Together, low-level and intermediate-level processing identifies areas of the image that are connected to an object as figures and areas that are not. The third stage, high-level visual processing, which unravels along the way from the primary visual cortex to the lower temporal cortex, establishes categories and meanings. Here the brain integrates visual information with relevant information from a variety of other sources and allows us to recognize specific objects, faces and scenes.

The relations between visual perception and graphic representation appear more evident when reading the commentary on the stages described by Kandel and reported by Tagliagambe (2005). Of these two stages, that of intermediate-level visual processing is considered particularly challenging because it requires the primary visual cortex to determine which segments belong to a single object and which are components of other objects in the context of a complex visual scene, composed of hundreds or even thousands of line segments. Here we see the crucial importance of the intermediate space and the boundary as a dividing line. Studies on the ways in which the visual world is organized for all species that can focus light to form images show that these modes must, in any case, be characterized by the presence of segregated figures that are distinct from the background. Given the properties of light, there are few ways to achieve this. One way, very general, is to obtain margins or edges where physical stimulation detects differences. The problem, of course, is that in many circumstances these physical variations can be very little clear, not to say indistinct, or they can be present only at times (think of an animal moving in the dense foliage). So, by means of natural selection, interpolation mechanisms have been developed which, using rather simple rules based on the statistical regularity of the environment (similarity of colour, clarity and texture, continuity of direction, common movement of the parts, etc.) extract margins and demarcation lines.

It is recognized in this assessment of the contours of the forms on the basis of 'statistical regularity of the environment'—such as colour, clarity, texture, continuity of direction, common movement of the parts, etc.—aimed at the extraction of the lines, the fulcrum on which the entire process of graphic representation is based, i.e. the coding through the lines of the contrasts perceived in the environment and their composition on the plane of representation. As Ching (1990) writes that a line can be conceived as a two-dimensional element characterized by length but without thickness or depth. Such a line does not actually exist. We perceive as lines the contours created by discontinuity on planes, surfaces, colours or textures. In drawing the images we perceive or visualize, we rely mainly on lines to visually communicate shapes. The line, therefore, exists as a fundamental element of drawing.

The plan of the representation is by definition two-dimensional on which a point, line or surface takes on precise spatial qualities. By placing a point or line in one position or another on the plane, with reference to the edge of the painting, they create different spatial fields as a dynamic moving form. The elements take on dynamic connotations depending on their respective position in the plane. The optical units take on energy and direction, becoming spatial forces (Kepes 1986). Positions, directions and differences in size, shape, clarity, colour and texture are evaluated and assimilated by the eye, producing a different kind of experience also and above all because they are all on the same flat surface, the plane of representation (Massironi 1989).

This process of organizing visual stimuli explained through the laws of form derived from Gestalt studies, makes one perceive the relationships between the parts of the image rather than the visual units as isolated entities. As optical illusions show, we do not see isolated fractions of a given observed subject, but our vision depends on the relationships between the parts and only later on the individual stimuli produced by the elements are considered autonomously. For this reason, colours, shapes, dimensions and more generally all the characteristics of the elements as perceived also depend on the characteristics of the immediately adjacent elements. Each visual unit acquires its own way of appearing through a dynamic interrelation with the surrounding optical environment. Unconsciously we try to organize and perceive in an organic whole the different sensations aroused by the optical qualities and measures and in doing so we are induced, depending on the nature of their reciprocal relationships and those with the plane of representation, to attribute particular spatial meanings to these relationships. Every optical difference on the pictorial surface generates a sensation by virtue of the procedure with which the eye organizes it within the system perceived in a unitary way (Kepes 1986).

According to the approach of the theory of form, the perception of the image occurs through the mutual action of external physical forces and internal forces of the individual. External forces are the light agents that strike the eye and produce reactions on the retina. The internal forces constitute the dynamic tendency of the individual to find a form of equilibrium after every input coming from the outside, trying to maintain in this way the system in conditions of relative stability. Every external impulse on the eye is thus counterbalanced by a reaction from within. The changes produced by light on the retina are balanced by physiological reactions so that the eye, or rather the neuro-muscular apparatus, always finds a new equilibrium (de Sausmarez 1974).

Like any machine subjected to continuous and prolonged work, the eye also has physiological limits to its ability to work, overcoming which it enters a condition of stress. These limits of visual experience are imposed by the nervous system. Perceptive attention is limited in particular by two factors: the first is the rather low number of optical units that can be embraced instantly and jointly; the second is the short duration of the eye's focusing time on a given static optical situation. Observing numerous, complex and disorganized systems of visual elements is difficult, as well as observing a static relationship for a long time without losing interest. In order for the image to remain alive, the relationships between the elements within the image must be able to keep the attention of the perceiver on (Massironi 1998).

The ultimate scope of the plastic organization is a structure of movement that progressively pushes to identify new spatial relationships until the experience reaches its fullest spatial saturation. The organization of the graphic elements is translated by the perceptive act into an ocular movement. This neuro-muscular movement consumes nervous energies that also require resting spaces. The relation and alternation of activity and rest generates the perceptive rhythm. To dilate the field and time of attention, the representation must have a rhythmically articulated organizational structure.

Although rhythmic organization is an essential condition for retaining attention and thus prolonging the life limits of the image, it is not entirely sufficient on its own to ensure the maximum duration of interest. A rhythmic model has a regularity that can become monotonous. The eye and mind must be nourished with visual stimuli designed to guide perception along a predefined path that can prolong attention and not tire the gaze. Within this field of attention, we can see clearly and simultaneously only a limited number of visual units. In the presence of a complex optical field, we will activate a series of strategies of the gaze aimed at bringing complexity back to simpler visual systems. These strategies have been analyzed and theorized through the laws of Gestalt's grouping of visual elements.

2.4 Graphic Representation—Visual Perception

To represent graphically means to transmit messages through the visual channel using images and words (Kroeger 2008), considering the latter not for their meaning but for their signifier and therefore as a mere graphic sign. Through graphic representation, graphic products are constructed that relate drawn sets of signs capable of acquiring particular meanings.

From visual perception and its mechanisms derive the strategies of graphic representation that allow to use perceptive mechanisms also to adequately codify messages (Massironi 1989). If you look to the decoding paths, it is, in fact, possible to identify what are the coding strategies of such signs for the transmission of messages through the visual channel.

As already mentioned, the image originates from the light energy that flows through the eye of the observer to his nervous system, recreating the sensations of light and colour through the perception of optical qualities. The geometric demarcation generated by these qualities constitutes the physical basis for the perception of spatial configurations. The perceived geometric demarcations thus give life to the elements of graphic language. By combining the primary elements, which we can compare to the alphabet of a language, what can be called secondary elements, i.e. the words of the graphic language, are formed. The infinite compositions born from the union of these last ones give life to the representations that are the equivalent of the sentences of a language and that allow to communicate even complex messages (Dondis 1973).

If it is true that visual perception starts from the unity of the whole and then only later decomposes into elementary parts and relations, graphic representation as an act of codification can only follow the inverse path and build itself through the composition and relation of the elementary parts into a unitary whole. Thus, the exploratory path of graphic representation can only start from the fundamental elements from which more complex elements originate. Point, line and background surface, i.e. the plane of the representation in which the graphic elements are composed, are the primary elements of the graphic representation (Kandinsky 1999).

2.4.1   Graphic Coding

The imprint of an instrument suitable for the purpose and driven by a man left on any surface generates the elementary optical unit, the primary element of graphic representation: the point. The point is the smallest perceptive unit that our eye can grasp. The sequence of points then defines the line, obtained from the trace of an instrument on the plane of representation. When the line moves freely in space enclosing and separating the plane of representation in two parts it defines a contour (Arnheim 2000) that divides the plane of representation into two surfaces, a figure and a background. The greater the variety and distinction between figure and background, and thus the contrast between their qualities, the more comprehensible a character can be as an individual expression or sign. The perception and representation of any image are based on this dynamic dualism.

By combining these primary elements, which we can compare to the alphabet of a language—the graphic language—we thus realize what can be defined as the words of that language: surfaces, shapes, background and figure, textures. The infinite compositions of these elements then give life to images that are the equivalent of the phrases of a language and that allow even complex messages to be communicated. Points and lines can then be further combined to form graphic motifs capable of distinguishing and characterizing surfaces and different perceptive effects. These are textures or patterns (Massironi 1989).

By manipulating the various elements—dots, lines, contours, shapes, surfaces— by varying their characters and relations—position, proportion, colour, value, texture, etc.—you achieve the same result as if you were composing the letters of the alphabet in countless combinations to form words that express meanings. In the same way, you can compose the graphic elements in countless combinations so that each particular relationship that is generated between them is able to stimulate a different spatial sensation.

Although the signs of graphic language are discreet elements, each of which has its own signifier and meaning—which in the case of visual communication becomes perception—the interpretation of meanings takes place on the basis of their unitary composition rather than individual elements, just as happens in verbal language. As already illustrated above, when one observes a work, be it architecture or a simple image, one perceives it first of all as a whole, as a unity.

Visual stimuli are analyzed as a whole, not as a simple sum of the individual parts. The perception of each part is influenced by its surroundings. The individual parts interact with each other and it is possible to modify these interactions so as to vary the overall perception. The image has an organic unity (Kepes 1986), i.e. it is a whole whose behaviour is not determined by that of its individual components, but in which the parts themselves are conditioned by the intrinsic nature of the whole. According to the Gestalt theory, perception is a global fact that depends on the context before being an analytical process of detail and the meaning of an element changes in relation to the sphere in which it is inserted. Unity means formal coherence between all the elements of the project to which the harmony, proportion, balance of the different elements that make it up to contribute (Elam 2001). Descartes already pointed out how in works composed of different parts and made by the hands of different creators there is less perfection than in those on which the only one worked.

So we see that large buildings, started and completed by a single architect, are usually more beautiful and harmonious than those that many have tried to renovate using old walls built for other purposes. That's why the ancient cities that, born from simple hamlets, have become little by little big cities, mostly are so disharmonious in comparison to those, meeting regularity criteria, that an engineer, following his inspiration, traces them in a plain. And if even the individual buildings, taken one by one, often reveal no lesser, or even greater, artistic merits, however, to see how they are arranged, here a large one, there a small one, and how they make the streets curved and irregular, one would say they are put there in that way by chance rather than by the will of reasonable men (Descartes 1998).

All elements must appear as if they belonged to a single project and were not inserted randomly. In order to obtain unity in the graphic representation composed by its nature of heterogeneous elements, even very different ones, it is necessary to focus the attention on the whole design as much as and more than on the single elements that compose it. All the choices and relationships that are created between the forms must be aimed at creating unity between the individual parts through the use of strategies such as proximity, similarity, repetition and variation, continuity; strategies that not by chance follow the laws of the form already illustrated in the path of decoding the image through visual perception (White 2002). Unity, in fact, can be obtained through proximity because the elements that are positioned close together are perceived as being in relation to each other. Vice versa, the further away they are, the more they are considered to be conceptually distant from each other. Unity can also be achieved through the use of visual similarities, both in the structure of the overall design and in the single elements that compose it. Similarity can, for example, be achieved through the use of colour, shapes, dimensions, positions, alignments or textures. Or, again, unity can be determined by the use of repetition, which in turn can be obtained by acting on positions, dimensions, colour, the use of rules, backgrounds and squares. Repetition produces rhythm. Rhythm can be generated by the regular alternation or orderly repetition of figures, positions, distances, angles, curves, directions, intervals, solids and voids. Blanks, voids, should be considered elements of the graphic representation in the same way as full spaces. They have the function of constructing, suggesting and guiding the path of the observer's gaze (de Sausamrez 1974).

Graphic representation is a spatial art that presupposes the organization of elements in space, an articulation of solids and voids in space. Empty and full are the founding elements of graphic representation. The best way to focus attention on an element is to make the surrounding space empty. The drawing of the void allows to draw full spaces by focusing the observer's attention on certain parts of the plane and inviting the eye to read the representation according to predefined paths. In fact, the eye follows a particular path; the kinetic sensation of the movement of the eye makes perception a dynamic experience that also takes shape in the directions of the visual flow on the plane of representation.

An examination of the most successful graphics (whether they are posters, parts of brochures, covers, pamphlets, catalogues, banners, etc.) explains the reason for their fascination: the harmonious distribution of drawings and photos, print parts, spots of colour, stylised elements, is the eternal play between empty and full, between dark and light, between space and figure. It is the fascination of drawing that is the rhythm of lines, it is the message of pictograms and the conciseness of ideograms. A graphic artist, however, is also a person who layouts a magazine or a book. Even in this case, even though it does not appear in the finished work, there is a basic drawing; the paste-up of a magazine or illustrated magazine page is a schematic drawing, but still a drawing in which one must take into account white spaces, harmony of lines and masses, the airiness of the print with respect to the illustration and vice versa, the rhythm of the composition of the various aesthetically compared parts.

The graphic design must be read in an order consistent with the meaning of the project itself and the observer must find an access point. Each project should have a primary visual element, a focal point that can dominate the designed space; the observer who finds a starting point in reading the project is easily guided to the other information levels. Different levels of image reading can be organized by establishing hierarchies through the definition of particular dominance relationships that can be obtained by creating differences in scale, or by positioning, colour, style or shape. It must be taken into account that the lack of dominance in a group of elements to which the same weight is given creates competition between them and that the overall balance is obtained when the elements that are composed are numerically consistent. If the composition lacks hierarchy and contrast, the general effect may appear as background noise, a uniform and homogeneous texture that makes the composition a continuous and constant full.

The ocular movement is based not only on the perception of the existing elements, lines, contours of the figures, but also on the latent contours of the intervals between these figures. A sort of psychological completion of the optical intervals will make up for this with latent lines capable of playing the same organizational role in the actual lines. In accordance with the law of closure, intervals of values and colours can emerge in shapes, intervals of lines in figures, intervals of points in lines, generating new figures with new kinetic contours (Kanisza 1980).

References

R. Arnheim, *Arte e percezione visiva* (Feltrinelli, Milano, 2000)

F.K. Ching, *Drawing: A Creative Process* (Wiley, London, 1990)

M. de Sausmarez, *Basic Design: The Dynamics of Visual Form* (Studio Vista, London, 1974)

R. Descartes, *Discorso sul metodo* (Laterza, Roma-Bari, 1998)

A.D. Dondis, *A Primer of Visual Literacy* (MIT Press, Massachussets, 1973)

U. Eco, *La, ricerca della lingua perfetta nella cultura europea* (Laterza, Roma-Bari, 1993)

K. Elam, *Geometry of Design* (Princeton Architectural Press, New York, 2001)

E.R. Kandel, *L'età dell'inconscio: Arte, mente e cervello dalla grande Vienna ai nostri giorni* (Raffaello Cortina, Milano, 2012)

W. Kandinsky, *Punto linea superficie* (Adelphi, Milano, 1999)

G. Kanizsa, *Grammatica del vedere* (Il Mulino, Bologna, 1980)

G. Kepes, *Il linguaggio della visione* (Dedalo, Bari, 1986)

M. Kroeger, *Paul Rand: Conversation with Students* (Princeton Architectural Press, New York, 2008)

M. Massironi, *Vedere con il disegno* (Franco Muzzio, Padova, 1989)

M. Massironi, *Fenomenologia della percezione visiva* (Il Mulino, Bologna, 1998)

S. Tagliagambe, *Le, due vie della percezione e l'epistemologia del progetto* (Franco Angeli, Milano, 2005)

A.W. White, *The Elements of Graphic Design* (Allworth Press, New York, 2002)

Chapter 3
Graphic Intelligence

As we have introduced in previous chapters, Gardner seems to open the way for the definition and deepening of that graphic intelligence. Graphic intelligence requires all the forms of intelligence already illustrated in the previous paragraphs and belonging to the large family of visual-spatial skills (McKim 1972). Through perception, we know and acquire useful information to structure the problem to which the graphic intelligence is called to respond. Through visualization it is possible to elaborate the mental images that then, through the graphic skills, it will be possible to represent and, in representing them, to favour the production of new knowledge. Not only that, since drawing, besides being understood as an image and form of thought, is also an action (Cervellini 2013), it is necessary to highlight the gestural component and therefore the indispensable connections with the kinaesthetic intelligence on which every form of movement and coordination between mind and body depends. An amalgamation of intelligences that deserves to be explored, deepened and understood through the lens of multiple intelligences that allows us to analyze a theme, that of graphic representation, already widely discussed and addressed in the literature and in the disciplinary debate to which this volume tries to give a contribution.

3.1 Graphic Intelligence: A Definition

In general, *intelligence* is defined as the ability to solve problems, or to create products which are appreciated within one or more cultural context. It has been widely discussed and demonstrated that there are many human intellectual skills relatively autonomous that in the theory of multiple intelligences are called 'human intelligences', the number of which is neither irrefutably fixed nor universally recognized (Gardner 1983). In fact, rather than being rigidly distinct and defined, the different kinds of intelligence form a *continuum*. Therefore, these *intelligences* are 'fictions', namely scientific constructs potentially useful to illuminate scientific problems. Every human intellectual skill involves a set of problem-solving abilities that allow the individual to solve problems or difficulties in which he is undefeated and

E. Cicalò, *Graphic Intelligence*, SpringerBriefs in Applied Sciences and Technology, https://doi.org/10.1007/978-3-030-45244-5_3

if so, to create an effective product. Also, it involves the ability to find or create problems, in this way preparing the ground to the acquisition of new knowledge" (Gardner 1983). Applying this definition to the graphic skills, it emerges that they can and should actually be considered an autonomous form of intelligence. So far, in the literature, such skills have been instead assimilated to other broader intellectual human abilities such as *spatial intelligence* (Gardner 1983) and *visual intelligence* (Ferguson 1978). Actually, they also are considered an amalgam of skills, to the point that in this area of research the word *visual* often comes to be used as a synonym of *spatial,* because spatial human's intelligence is closely related to the observation of the environment. Therefore, in this continuum of human intelligence, we can identify, confine and define the *graphic intelligence*, which is certainly in close relation with other forms of intelligence and particularly with the spatial and the visual one (Fig. 3.1).

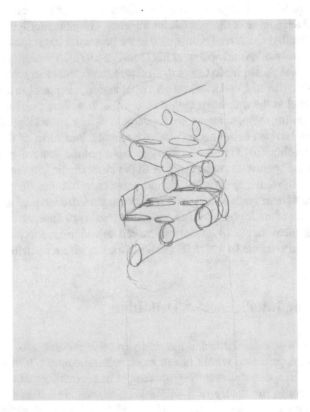

Fig. 3.1 Sketch of the DNA double helix, Francis Crick, 1953. The Francis Crick Papers http:// wellcomelibrary.org

The spatial intelligence is based on the ability of individuals to perceive the world and to operate on the basis of such perceptions. According to Gardner, it includes skills very different from each other, as the ability to perceive visually, to represent graphically and to create mental images through imagination. These are capacities related but distinct from each other and thus deserving of being analyzed independently. Howard Gardner writes that it is possible that these operations are independent from each other and that they can be developed or damaged separately. Nevertheless, like rhythm and melody cooperate with each other in music, the previously mentioned capacities typically occur together within the space. Actually, they operate as a family, and each skill may well enhance by the other. These spatial skills are used in various different fields. They are important for the orientation in different situations, from enclosed areas to oceans; relies on them the recognition of objects and scenes, both when they are in their original context and when it has changed. This form of intelligence is also used when working on graphical representations—two-dimensional or three-dimensional versions of scenes from the real world—as well as in connection with other symbols, such as in geographical or topographical maps, diagrams or geometric figures (Gardner 1983).

However, in discussing the spatial development of intelligence in different evolutionary stages, since the Piaget studies, Gardner recognizes how the different components of the amalgam of skills that he defines as *spatial intelligence* are developed independently. Indeed, children develop rapidly spatial understanding, but the representation of this knowledge involves an additional and different range of difficulties (Piaget and Inhelder 1948). The expression of this understanding through a symbolic code is more difficult. Therefore, another kind of intelligence seems to distinguish itself from the spatial one and to become useful and necessary to codify the understanding: the *graphic intelligence*, precisely.

The *graphic intelligence* can be defined as the ability to use drawing skills and, more generally, the ability to integrate the use of eye, mind and hand—i.e. perception, thinking and representation—to solve problems and create effective products aimed at acquiring new knowledge (Fig. 3.2).

Although the relationship between drawing and thought has already been the subject of studies (Van Sommers 1984; Goldshmidt 1991; Verstijnen and Hennessey 1998; Treib 2008), in the literature the concept of graphic intelligence has so far been studied mainly as a part of more complex forms of intelligence, like the spatial and visual intelligence already described and the *design intelligence* (Cross 1986). The *Thinking Hand* by Pallasmaa (2009), the *Graphic Thinking* by Laseau (1980), *Thinking with a Pencil* by Nelms (1964) and *The Mind's Eye* by Ferguson (1978) describe the different possibilities of combinations and integration of the three elements eye-mind-hand. The *graphic intelligence* can be defined as the ability to address and resolve problems through the coordination of eye, mind and hand—namely perception, thinking and representation—in the way in which we have seen Galileo observing, understanding and representing —not necessarily in this order—the lunar

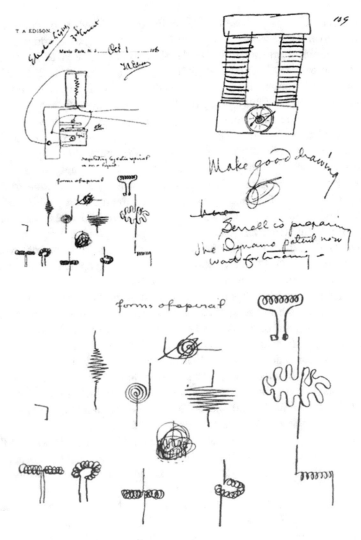

Fig. 3.2 Sketch of work on lamp filament light bulb, Thomas Edison, 1880 circa. The Thomas Edison Papers http://edison.rutgers.edu/

surface; developing that scientific imagination that Bruno Latour calls 'thinking with the eyes and hands' (Latour 1990), that is at the basis of the visualization process and of the making visible through graphic representation.

Thinking with eyes and hands, dealing with problematic situations proceeding through graphic experiments (Schön 1993), is not only constitutive of design disciplines, but actually underlies the development of thought in much broader disciplines and domains embracing the entire science and, as we shall see, beyond.

Smith (1964) claims that after a person has achieved adequate verbal expertise, his progress in science is determined by his spatial ability. As Gardner writes, very developed spatial intelligence is an invaluable resource. In some activities this skill is essential: as the case of sculptors or mathematical topologists; but there are many other fields in which the only spatial intelligence might not be enough to produce competence (Gardner 1983). Moreover, the *graphic intelligence* differs both from that spatial discussed by Gardner and from the visual one discussed by Robertson and even before by Arnheim (1969), according to whom the visual images are not only a useful aid to the thought but even their primary source. The most important operations of thought rely directly on our perception of the world. Onsight are based and are constituted our cognitive processes. Truly productive thinking in any area of cognition, Arnheim writes, takes place within the visual imagination. Enhancing the role of vision, he minimizes that of language. Only explicating by image processes or concepts, he argues, it is possible to think clearly about them. Consequently, visual and spatial intelligence contribute significantly to scientific and artistic thinking (Gardner 1983). Of the same opinion was Albert Einstein that, thinking in pictures, came to hypothesize his fundamental discoveries that, as he recognizes, are derived more from spatial thought that from purely mathematical reasoning. As he explained, the words of the language, both written and spoken, do not seem to have any role in his mechanism of thought. The psychological entities that seem to serve as elements in thought are certain signs and images more or less clear which can be voluntarily reproduced or combined. The factors mentioned above are, in his case, of visual and of muscular type (Gardner 1983). However, the ability to produce mental images may not be sufficient. There are situations in which reasoning by images allows us to solve a problem or achieve a cognitive result otherwise unachievable. At this point comes into play the drawing, the most suitable tool for the transmission of this type of knowledge (Massironi 1989) and, therefore, that *graphic intelligence* able to translate mental images through drawn images (Fig. 3.3).

Fig. 3.3 Sketch of work on optics, Isaac Newton, c. 1670–c. 1710. Cambridge Digital Library https://cudl.lib.cam.ac.uk

References

R. Arnheim, *Visual Thinking* (University of California Press, Berkeley, 1969)

F. Cervellini, Disegno - la parola - è un patrimonio. in ed. by A. Conte, M. Filippa, Patrimoni e Siti UNESCO: Memoria (Misura e Armonia, Roma, Gangemi, 2013)

A. Cross, Design intelligence: the use of codes and language systems in design. Des. Stud. (1986)

E.S. Ferguson, The mind's eye: nonverbal thought in technology. Science (1978)

H. Gardner, *Frames of Mind: The Theory of Multiple Intelligence*; (Basic Books, New York, NY, USA, 1983)

G. Goldschmidt, The dialectics of sketching. Creativity Res. J. (1991)

P. Laseau, *Graphic Thinking for Architects and Designers* (Van Nostrand Reinhold, New York, 1980)

B. Latour, Drawing Things Together, in *Representation in Scientific Practice*, ed. by M. Lynchm, S. Woolgar (MIT press, Cambridge, MA, 1990)

M. Massironi, *Vedere con il disegno* (Franco Muzzio, Padova, 1989)

R.H. McKim, *Experiences in Visual Thinking* (Brooks/Cole, Monterey, CA, 1972)

H. Nelms, *Thinking with a Pencil* (Bernes & Noble, London, 1964)

J. Pallasmaa, *The Thinking Hand: Existential and Embodied Wisdom in Architecture* (Wiley, Chichester, 2009)

J. Piaget, B. Inhelder, *La, représentation de l'espace chez l'enfant* (Presses Universitaires de France, Paris, 1948)

D.A. Schön, *Il professionista riflessivo. Per una nuova epistemologia della pratica professionale* (Edizioni Dedalo, Bari, 1993)

I.M. Smith, *Spatial Ability: Its Educational and Social Significance* (University of London Press, London, 1964)

M. Treib, *Drawing/Thinking: Confronting in an Electronic Age* (Routledge, London, New York, 2008)

P. Van Sommers, *Drawing and Cognition: Descriptive and Experimental Studies of Graphic Production Processes* (Cambridge University Press, New York, NY, USA, 1984)

I.M. Verstijnen, J.M. Hennessey, Sketching and creative discovery. Des. Stud. (1998)

Chapter 4
Graphic Intelligence in Scientific Investigation

In this chapter is presented and discussed the hypothesis of a particular form of intelligence, in the context of the theories on the multiple intelligences: the *graphic intelligence*, intended as the capacity to use the drawing skills and, more generally, the ability to integrate the use of eye, mind and hand to solve problems and to create effective products aimed to acquiring new knowledge.

Indeed, the recent research from the cognitive sciences suggests the existence of a meaningful relationship between graphic representation and cognitive development that could support the idea of a *graphic intelligence* autonomous from other forms of intelligence that have until now been considered capable of describing and comprehend this type of human intellectual competence. Thus, the *graphic intelligence* could be equally confronted with the most common linguistic and logical-mathematical intelligence, on which nowadays school tends to focus, and it could complete and enrich the already investigated visual and spatial intelligence. Thinking of the graphic skills as form of intelligence obliges to turn the attention not on the product but on the cognitive process that led to the elaboration of that product. This means a change of perspective able to suggest new approaches to teaching at all levels and in all the fields of education.

As discussed in the previous chapters, Gardner (1983) defines as *intelligence* the ability to solve problems or to create products appreciated in a cultural context. According to his theory on multiple intelligences, intellective human competences are various, relatively autonomous and their nature and their articulation are not definable, because they tend to shape themselves and to combine among them in a variety of adaptive ways. Indeed, they form a *continuum,* rather than being distinct in a rigid and definite manner. Therefore, every type of intelligence, thought as isolated and autonomous, configure themselves as 'fictions', or scientific constructs potentially useful to explore scientific issues. Using this explorative strategy, Gardner identifies seven main types of intelligence: the linguistic intelligence, the logical-mathematical intelligence, the musical intelligence, the spatial intelligence, the bodily-kinaesthetic, the intrapersonal intelligence and the interpersonal intelligence.

E. Cicalò, *Graphic Intelligence*, SpringerBriefs in Applied Sciences and Technology, https://doi.org/10.1007/978-3-030-45244-5_4

Starting from the previously described definition of intelligence, Gardner claims that many problems are not solvable through linguistic or logical-mathematical propositions, but—mainly in the fields of images and spatial objects—they need to be considered as a problem of visual imagination. This ability is traditionally separated from those logic-mathematical and linguistic and it is often defined 'the other intelligence'. This is the spatial intelligence, based on non-verbal languages and opposed, but at the same time complementary, to the intelligences based on verbal languages.

The spatial intelligence has been defined by Howard Gardner as the composition of different skills connected among them. They work as a family and are able to support each other. The ability to recognize images of the same object, the ability to visually transform an object in another or to recognize this transformation, as well as the skill to make a graphic representation of the spatial information belong to this family. Thus, the graphic skills would be part of the spatial intelligence and it would be also the basis of the ability to represent, in two or three dimensions, the real world by using symbolic codes, as in the case of geographic and topographic representations, diagrams and geometric figures.

Consequently, the research of Gardner introduces another form of intelligence that is responsible of the graphic expression of spatial concepts: this is the graphic intelligence or the skill to use the graphic abilities, and more, in general, the coordination of eyes, mind and hands—perception, cognition and representation—in order to solve problems and to make effective results for the generation of new knowledge.

4.1 Graphic Representation as an Explorative Tool

In our culture and in our educative system the concept of graphic representation is mostly linked to the idea of artistic making to which is attributed a quality mainly—if not exclusively—from the aesthetical point of view; that is referred to its ability to represent and make recognizable a subject. Instead, the quality referred to different processes, as those cognitive, is mostly recognized in the field of design education, and it is based on an idea of drawing intended as an exploratory process. These are, of course, two different and almost antithetical conceptions of image widespread in our culture: the image as representation and the image as cognitive and knowledge process, the first of which largely predominant on the second.

Theories, techniques, graphic and artistic methods should not be considered solely functional to the production of images representing the reality, but it should be seen also—and mainly—as tools for the strengthening of thought. Indeed, images worth not only as a product, that is as the final result of a graphic elaboration but also an expression of the cognitive processes made possible by and in the act of the production that image (Figs. 4.1 and 4.2).

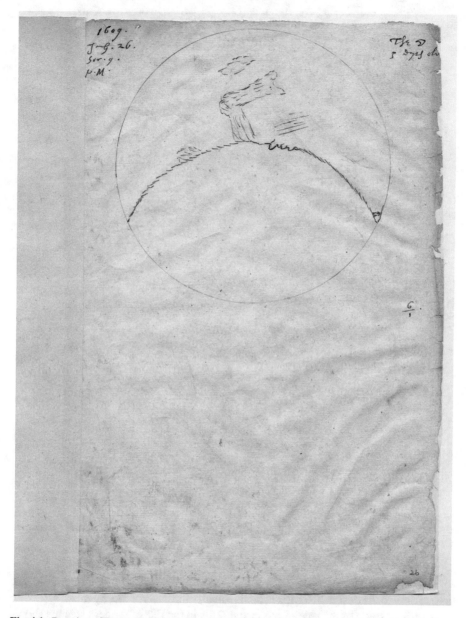

Fig. 4.1 Drawing of the moon, Thomas Harriot, 1609. West Sussex Record Office Online Catalogue
http://www.westsussexpast.org.uk

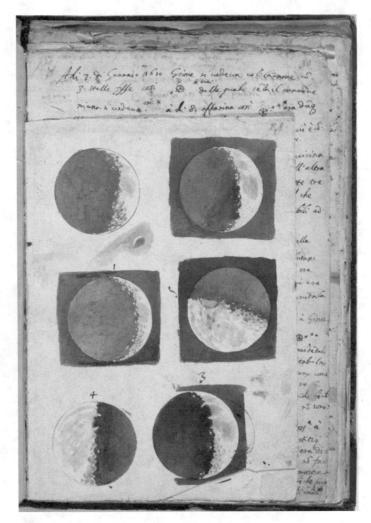

Fig. 4.2 Drawing of the moon, Galileo Galilei, 1609. Biblioteca Nazionale Centrale di Firenze
http://www.bncf.firenze.sbn.it

This different value of the image as a tool for thought strengthening does not belong only to the design disciplines but is actually the basis of more general scientific thought. The study of the role of the visual skills in the rise of modern science shows that the aesthetic dimension of image is not the main issue for scientists who produced them. Indeed, historians of science assign to image and to graphic representation a key role in scientific progress, considering them as fundamental factors in the rise of modern science (Baldasso 2006).

As the history of science explains, graphics representations have been, and still are, fundamental for the achievement and the formulation of discoveries because they are essential to define the characteristics of the phenomena observed in nature or often only intuited. One paradigmatic example can be found in the Sidereus Nuncius, published in 1610 by Galileo Galilei; a short treatise on astronomy on observations and discoveries destined to revolutionize not only the entire cosmology but also the method of scientific research and of dissemination and communication of the research results. The images printed in this book are generally considered as the precursors of infographics. However, they are appreciated more for their aesthetic quality that for those cognitive whose understanding needs to consider the historical and scientific context.

Galileo was not the first scientist to observe the phenomena that would have then allowed him to formulate his revolutionary theories. As written by Renzo Baldasso, a few weeks before him—the sources speak of two and a half lunar cycles—another scientist, Thomas Harriot, had preceded him (Bredekamp 2001). The two scientists observed the same phenomena with different instruments. Both were able to formulate an interpretation of what was observed, and both used the graphic representation as a tool of visualization, understanding and communication of the observed phenomena. However, it is clear that there are deep differences in their ability to use techniques, tools and methods of graphic representation as tools of thought. The Harriot representations show the moon as a lighted ball whose boundary between light and shadow is irregular but not able to represent the actual shape of the Moon's surface. In contrast, Galileo draws a pattern of lights and shadows corresponding to quite pronounced irregularities in the lunar surface structure.

Therefore, Galileo grasps and transmits something that Harriot was not able to visualize. Actually, for Galileo, that problem was not new at all. Indeed, many years before in Florence, Galileo had learned the theory of secondary light for which the effects of light are reflected less intensely on other surfaces. Then, perhaps it is not an insignificant detail that Galileo was taught, round 1585, by Ostilio Ricci, the mathematician of the Medici court which then also became a teacher at the Accademia del Disegno in Florence, in the home of the artist and engineer Bernardo Buontalenti, to which Galileo was later admitted (Bredekamp 2001).

Viviani gives evidence of the talent of Galileo for the art of drawing and writes that at that time his aspirations were precisely the ones to make painting his profession (Viviani 1890). Then, these abilities are fully expressed right in Siderius Nuncius, where the graphic representations drew by Galileo show not only a high precision but also a mastery of techniques that allowed him to render the plasticity of the lunar surface. This ability to read and represent lights and shadows was fundamental to the interpretation of the heights and depths of the lunar surface (Edgertone 1984).

Education in science and mathematics was at that time a key part of artist training. The Ostilio Ricci class not only were about the perspective but also the fundamentals of geometry. As evidenced by Bredekamp, the Galileo ability to calculate and visualize the configuration of the lunar surface can be connected to the lessons in the scientific tracts used at the time, as the *Perspectiva Corporum Regularu* (Bredekamp 2001). Galileo was able to reconnect his observations to a simple problem learned in the math class for artists: the relationship between a pattern of lights and shadows and a morphology of heights and depths. Thus, taking advantage of his knowledge of the techniques and of the scientific theories of the graphical representation, Galileo was able to view and make viewable to the public his intuitions, as Harriot was not able to do.

The advantage of Galileo versus Harriot helps to explain how the ability to integrate seeing, thinking and drawing is essential in the cognitive process, but not only. This ability to solve problems through the coordination between eye, mind and hand can be called *graphic intelligence*, intended as an autonomous form of intelligence in the theories of multiple intelligences.

4.2 Thinking by Drawing in Science and Art

The natural scientists traditionally conduct their investigations through perception and direct observation of reality. Then, the activities of scientific research aim to isolate and imitate some aspects of observed processes. They are revealed using artificial objects able to reproduce, to communicate and to make understandable what has been observed. So that any subject may be more easily intelligible, it must be recognizable by our senses so that, thanks to the representation of its shape, that subject can be described and understood (Ferguson 1978). Many of the problems in which scientists and engineers are engaged cannot be described verbally. The morphological approach becomes one of the primary and fundamental steps of each discipline inherent in the natural sciences (Massironi 1989).

Since the Renaissance, it had been developed a scientific approach to the graphic representation to the point that some historians of science consider the history of art of this time as a fundamental chapter in the history of science (Butterfield 1954). Indeed, it is since the Renaissance that scientific progress has used graphic representations in order to record and to transmit knowledge and then, with the invention of printing, they could also spread, contributing substantially to the teaching of science and to the promotion of scientific thought (Gardner 1983). The subjects of these representations are not always the explicit forms of the observed objects but are often drawings that, rather than depict the visual perception of the object, grasps and tracks connections and interactions in relation to the available knowledge and to the possible verifications. Therefore, in the represented forms we should not look to the similarity with the visible features of objects and phenomena observed, but to the ability to represent the knowledge gained (Massironi 1989).

The relationship between the observation of phenomenon and the representation of knowledge is mediated by the production of mental images that are originated from the analysis of the studied reality and that are based on mental hypothesis rather than on visible evidence (Klee 1959). Proceeding by analogies is the basis of this mental process that we try to control through understandable and reassuring shapes. Graphic patterns are not entirely isomorphic representations.

They often recur to rhetorical artifices of verbal derivation—as in the case of the allegories, metaphors or visual metonymy—though they are never totally assimilated to them. Rather than depictions of specific objects or rhetorical artifices, Manfredo

Massironi speaks of *ipotetigrafia*, defined as 'the graphic product that helps to give visual form to the hypothesis made to explain the behaviour or the functioning of natural conditions intuited or experimentally observed and of which it constitutes an explanatory model' (Massironi 1989). The progress in science may be very closely associated to the development of this type of representation. Indeed, many scientific theories are based on graphical representations: the tree of life Darwin, the notion of Freud's submerged unconscious, the Dalton concept of the atom, the structure of the DNA molecule proposed by James Watson and Francis Crick, the ring pattern of Kekule benzene, the graphical notation of the vector of Hamilton. These are all images that Massironi defines productive since they can give rise to key ideas in science and can help to conceive them (Fig. 4.3).

Fig. 4.3 Tree of life drawing, Charles Darwin, 1837. Darwin On Line http://darwin-online.org.uk/

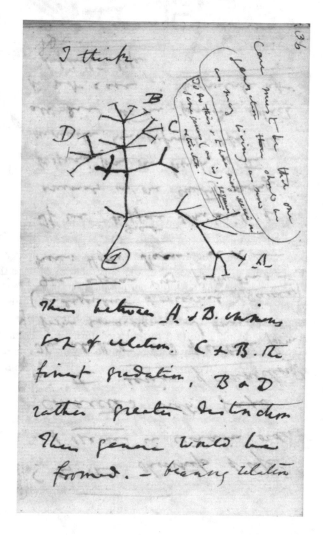

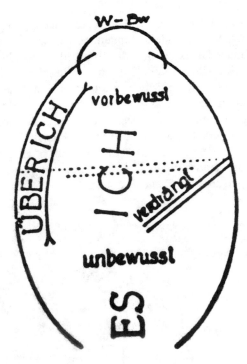

Fig. 4.4 Psyche diagram, Sigmund Freud, 1933. Sigmund Freud Archives http://www.
freudarchives.org

Sometimes these images are produced only in the minds of scientists, other times
they are materialized in models or translated on paper. Often the three visualization modes are integrated into a single cognitive process that crosses the different
dimensions until the result of the formulation of scientific discovery is achieved.
This process begins with the mental elaboration that the investigator pursues trying
to reorganize the data usually provided by measurements obtained using appropriate
equipment. These data fail to be understandable and communicable only if they are
synthesized into a unified formal structure and articulated that govern them. This
synthesis can be verified and communicated only if given 'visual', so making image,
representation of the studied phenomenon (Figs. 4.4 and 4.5).

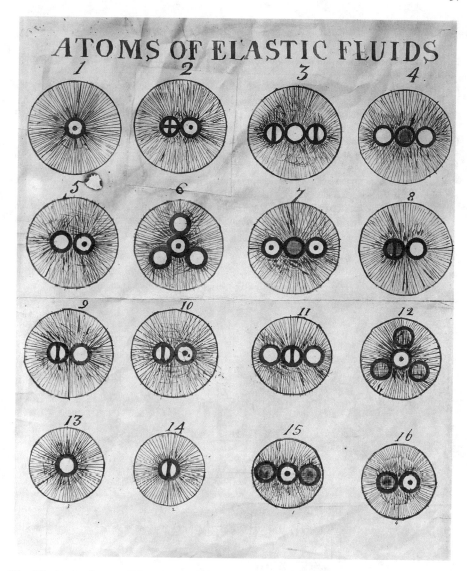

Fig. 4.5 Atoms diagram, John Dalton, 1806. https://wellcomeimages.org

References

R. Baldasso, The role of visual representation in the scientific revolution: a histographyc inquiry. Centaurus **48** (2006)

H. Bredekamp, Gazing hands and blind spots: galileo as draftsman. Sci. Context (2001)

H. Butterfield, Renaissance art and modern science. Univ. Rev. (1954)

S.Y. Edgerton Jr, Galileo, Florentine "disegno", and the "Strange Spottednesse" of the Moon. Art J. (1984)

E.S. Ferguson, The mind's eye: nonverbal thought in technology. Science (1978)

H. Gardner, *Frames of Mind: The Theory of Multiple Intelligence* (Basic Books, New York, NY, USA, 1983)

P. Klee, *Teoria della forma e della figurazione* (Feltrinelli, Milano, 1959)

M. Massironi, *Vedere con il disegno* (Franco Muzzio, Padova, 1989)

V. Viviani, Racconto istorico della vita del Sig. Galileo Galilei. in ed. by G. Galilei, *Opere di Galileo* (Barbera, Firenze, 1890). H. Bredekamp, Gazing Hands and Blind Spots, Galileo as Draftsman. Sci. Context (2001)

Chapter 5
Designing by Graphic Intelligence

The concept of graphic intelligence is certainly nothing new for those who are used to using this form of intelligence daily within their professions. Architects, engineers and, more generally, designers base their entire work activity on graphic thought, that form of thought that involves the hand, the eye and the brain in the elaboration and communication of design ideas (Gardner 1983).

During their training and experience, designers acquire a modus operandi that makes graphic language and graphic thought the privileged tools for the production of ideas and for the representation of the projects on which their professional activity focuses. For the designer, graphic intelligence corresponds to a concept of drawing understood simultaneously as thought, image and action (Cervellini 2013). The ability of designers to use drawing in parallel and at the same time alternatively with verbal language, their ability to translate mental images into graphic representation, that is the natural way in which they use graphic intelligence to communicate and express a thought, should be a fundamental objective not only in specialist training but also in generalist training. In fact, other fields of investigation such as the arts, literature, cinema and theatre are equally significant and illustrative of how graphic intelligence can be an essential tool in the most diverse professional fields.

5.1 Graphic Languages, Verbal Languages and Design Languages

The use of graphic intelligence as a tool for the elaboration of ideas is common to several disciplines. There are numerous links within theoretical discussions and interdisciplinary research that seek to make use of experiences from different fields of knowledge to strengthen and exemplify concepts, and that trace relevant analogies between methods of elaboration of ideas, the composition of elements and conception of works. It is interesting in this regard the parallelism between verbal and graphic languages that can be explored starting from Cicero's discussion on oratory art.

© The Author(s), under exclusive license to Springer Nature Switzerland AG 2020
E. Cicalò, *Graphic Intelligence*, SpringerBriefs in Applied Sciences
and Technology, https://doi.org/10.1007/978-3-030-45244-5_5

Oratory art, as well as a graphic representation, are in fact forms of communication based on the composition of primary elements: words composed in speeches, in the first case; graphic signs composed in representations, in the second. Cicerone claims that just as we do not need to constantly search again for individual letters every time we have to write a word, so it is not necessary to find new arguments reserved for a specific theme; rather, it is appropriate to have a certain repertory of general ideas which, like the letters to write the word, that immediately manifests themselves in our thoughts when we have to communicate. Similarly, in the graphic representation, you can acquire repertoires of signs that become available to address and solve specific problems.

Not dissimilar is the parallelism between words and graphic signs, between verbal and graphic language proposed by Mari (2008), who underlines how cursive writing, with its fluidity and the speed that distinguishes it, allows to almost instantly stop that flow of thought that our brain produces continuously in the same way as free-hand sketching, what Mari calls 'cursive drawing', allows to represent very quickly hundreds of hypotheses in a sufficiently descriptive way (Mari 2008), to graphically represent ideas in their becoming, to be materially coherent with the act of thinking that flows alternating words and images (Mari 2003). Mari writes that 'Thought, is a very rapid flow of fragments of memory... images... doubts... curiosity... hopes... fears... Billions of neurons are involved to give a useful answer to survival... "survival" is not an excessive word. For billions of years, every animal's need has been to survive on the condition that it can eat or be eaten. A matter of tenths of a second. Our brains have evolved to increase that speed. A myriad of information is involved, which is why it appears in the cheapest and fastest form possible: allusive images, elementary words, sensations' (Mari 2008). The drawing has the ability to grasp the thoughts in their rapid and continuous flow and to stop them on the paper is described by Ettore Sottsass: 'Thinking doesn't make noise or light. Thoughts are not heard or seen. When someone looks into the void, perplexed, the other asks, "What are you thinking?" […] In order to hear someone's thoughts, the idea of inventing words came to him. Someone thought that the sound of words could somehow represent the wandering of thoughts. […] Someone else had the idea of drawing signs to represent thoughts,—certain thoughts—with light, with something you can see' (Sottsass 2002). This parallelism between writing and drawing, between verbal and graphic languages and in particular between cursive writing and 'cursive drawing', can be found in some studies on the grammatical structure, semantics and syntax of graphic language (Herbert 1988, Stiny 1985, Laseau 1980, Alexander 1964, David 1972). However, the two languages, verbal and visual, are not similar but complementary languages. As Schön (1993) argues, drawing and speaking are parallel ways of designing and together they constitute the language of design.

5.2 Drawing in Design Process

According to the most widespread traditional conception, drawing would simply be a method of representation, but if its role were limited to this it would be easily supplanted today by new digital methodologies. Less is, instead, the awareness of how much is able to translate into signs the language of visual and creative thought: a real method of thinking (Brown 2008). Drawing is, therefore, a means, an instrument of thought, and not its finality (Dee 2008).

Drawing, especially designing to design, is a type of modelling that, as cognitivist psychology teaches us today, poses a series of questions that are anything but simple. Why drawing to design manifests itself at the same time as drawing during designing and designing during designing. It is this interacting co-presence between the medium (drawing) and the aim (designing) that allows us to advance towards the solution sought and sometimes only found (Maldonado 2005) (Fig. 5.1).

Drawing as a project tool establishes the coexistence, overlapping or even coincidence between drawing and project. To better understand this concept it is useful to refer to the description of the design action formulated by Donald Schön. A designer—Schön claims—creates things. Sometimes he makes the final product; more often, he makes a representation or an image of an artifact that others will have to build. He works in particular situations, uses particular materials, and employs distinctive expressive means and languages. Typically, his process of realization is complex. There are more variables—possible types of choices, norms and relationships between them—that can be represented in a finite model. Because of this complexity, the designer's actions tend, fortunately or unfortunately, to produce different consequences than those desired. When this happens, the designer can take into account the unintentional changes he has produced in the situation, generating new appreciation and understanding and making new choices. He shapes the situation in accordance with his initial appreciation of it, the situation 'replies', and he responds to the impertinent reply of the situation.

In a good design process, this conversation with the situation is reflective. In response to the replication of the situation, the designer reflects in the course of action on the construction of the problem, on the strategies of action, or on the model of phenomena, implicit in his actions (Schön 1993).

5.3 Problem-Solving by Freehand Drawing

The freehand drawing, in particular, is the tool that allows the designer an internal dialogue aimed at exploring the design complexity, at defining the problems connected to the project (Herbert 1988), the constraints connected to the contextual conditions, to arrive then at the hypothesis of design strategies to solve the same problems.

These constraints characterize the design practices and distinguish its representations from those proper to artistic practices (Treib 2008). Art has no constraints,

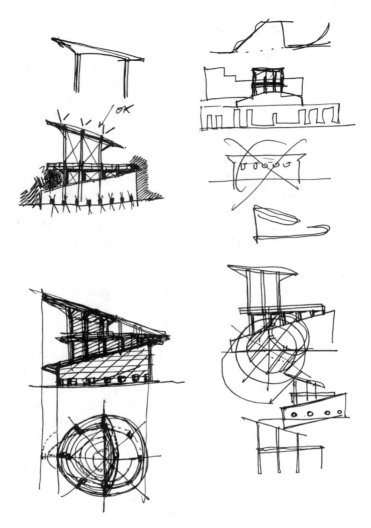

Fig. 5.1 Architectural sketching, Museo Archeologico di Olbia, Vanni Maciocco

it is an expression of absolute freedom, unlike design which have to take account of contextual, functional, economic and social constraints. These are the constraints that stimulate doubts and at the same time constitute the essence of design action as a process of exploration of complex problems in all fields and in all possible declinations. In this regard, significant are Igor Strawinsky's words describing the role of constraints in a musical composition: 'As far as concerns myself, I feel a kind of terror when, at the moment of getting to work and in front of the infinite possibilities offered to me, I have the feeling that everything is allowed. If everything is allowed to me, the best and the worst, if nothing resists me, every effort is inconceivable, I can't rely on anything to build and therefore every enterprise would be in vain. [...]

My freedom therefore consists in moving within the limited plan I have set myself for each of my enterprises' (Strawinsky 1942).

In the preliminary phase of the design process, the need to confront the constraints of action gives rise to abstract ideas which, despite their still high degree of indeterminacy and uncertainty, freehand drawing makes it possible to stop on paper (Gross et al. 1988). The act of drawing can be rapid and spontaneous, but the traces that remain are stable. The designer can examine them at his convenience, the speed of the action can be changed at any time, the designer can slow down, to think about what he is doing (Schön 1993). Once stopped and recorded, the images go through a cyclical and repetitive path of checks and variations that gradually address the complexity of the design subject and try to translate into the simplicity of the hypothesized solutions.

No move is irreversible. The designer can try, observe and switch to another sheet of paper, try again. As a result, he can perform learning sequences in which he corrects his mistakes and takes into account the results of his previously unplanned moves (Schön 1993).

'The solution is always hidden somewhere inside the problem, you just have to find it' (Kroeger 2008) and the drawing guides the designer in this research by favouring the extraction of thoughts and their translation into images. As Goldschmidt (1991) explains, design problems are 'badly-structured' and it is, therefore, necessary to conduct research towards a design solution because there are no problem-solving algorithms as in the case of 'well-structured' problems. The design research is first of all aimed at revealing valid preliminary ideas, a design concept that can be developed and refined into concrete design solutions. In the process of generating, developing and evaluating ideas, we reason about them: the designer or the project team investigates ideas and images, sources of inspiration, partial solutions so as to ensure their relevance, their confluence with the requirements and constraints and their mutual compatibility. In this way, the potential contribution of possible alternative pathways is established. The exploratory process requires that the ideas in question are represented so that one can react to them, transform them, refine them or set them aside. Since our cognitive apparatuses are provided with the capacity of imagination, we make extensive use of it in the design process: visual imagination is the place of internal representations where designers reach and nourish design hypotheses. However, imagination is restricted by several factors such as the clarity of images, their duration, our ability to read information and manipulate it. External representations are supposed to compensate for the limitations of internal representations, which explains why the designer uses external representations from the earliest stages of the design process. When the designer works in a team or is confronted with others, drawings are the necessary external representations because communication depends on them, but the dialogue the designer conducts with himself is no less meaningful (Goldschmidt 1991).

It is precisely this way of understanding design that allows the professional to reflect in the course of the action, dialoguing with the situations that arise from time to time during the design process. The drawing sheets are the expressive medium of reflection in the course of the action. Designers can draw and communicate their ideas in the language of spatial action, leaving traces that represent the shapes of buildings on site. Because drawing reveals qualities and relationships not previously imagined, the drawings can act as experiments (Schön 1993).

Alvaro Siza (1997), defining drawing as a form of communication with the self and with others, invites us to reflect on the two ways in which drawing is used by designers in their design processes: one connected to drawing as document and history of the formation of an architectural image, another connected to the organization of this image in the project according to a series of notations essentially aimed at communicating the project itself according to its correct execution. These two phases are not temporally consecutive and logically causal, but only functionally distinct, able to interact and influence each other during the whole process of project elaboration.

The drawing has a transitory nature, it is a link between the conception and the realization that is made through the use of various tools and at different scales crossing three levels of application (Treib 2008):

- at the conceptual level, it constitutes of a tool for dialogue between the designer and his ideas;
- at the communicative level, it becomes an instrument of dialogue between the designer and the other subjects involved in the decision-making phase;
- at the executive level, it acts as a tool for the definition of all the details necessary for communication between the designer and the executors.

For each level there are preferential tools to which to commit responsibility for the success of the individual phases, depending on whether one is looking for a qualitative or quantitative representation, whether one expects from it the communication of ideas or the measurement of dimensions, the presentation of the concepts or the quantification of the elements.

In observing the action of the students, Schön (1993) writes that in order to benefit from the drawing as an experimental medium, the designer must acquire certain skills and knowledge. He needs to learn the traditions of graphic media, languages, notations. Students have a repertoire of expressive media that allows them to choose the most suitable graphic method to explore a particular problem. Sketches allow him to explore the overall geometric order; cross-section drawings, to examine three-dimensional effects; scale drawings, to experiment with the dimensions of the design; models, to examine the relationships between constructive masses, their volumes, light and shadow. He uses the methods of expression selectively to approach the themes to which he gives priority at each stage of the design process (Schön 1993).

Drawing is, therefore, a versatile tool, capable of creating private as well as public representations. But this rigid distinction does not correspond to the real use made of design representations, which instead very often lead to the use of more private studies as a means of communication and the publication and dissemination of more technical works as well as preliminary sketches. Moreover, it should not be forgotten how these exploratory drawings are useful, if not necessary, even in the phases following the more strictly creative preliminary one. Because of its rapidity, or its practicality, sometimes because of its economy, expressiveness, or even its simplicity, drawing often becomes an indispensable tool even in the persuasive and executive spheres. Just as it is impossible to leave out the sketches made on site to support communication with the executors or the sketches used to give character to design drawings often made cold, inexpressive, or in any case unoriginal, by representations based on software.

The design is, therefore, a tool that has great versatility, both within the more private sphere of dialogue between the designer and the project, and in the public sphere of communication between the designer and the other stakeholders involved in the decision-making, design and executive process.

5.4 Drawing in the Idea Production Process

The design studies conducted through freehand drawing seem spontaneous, informal and completely random. In reality, they originate from the re-elaboration of a large amount of pre-processed information coming from previous perceptive and cognitive processes. The project studies, the sketches, are based on a hidden structure of relationships that originates from a process of abstraction, that is, of selection and organization of information. Each project process is based on a large amount of 'raw' information coming from the context conditions, suggested by the project program, accumulated in previous experiences, which are subjected to a process of abstraction, or rather of organization functional to be then used to achieve a set purpose (Herbert 1988).

The ideas are a combination of pre-existing elements whose elaboration depends on the ability to see the possible relations between them (Young 2003). The formulation of ideas as defined by Young, therefore, requires a previous collection and a fundamental absorption of 'raw material': images, information, examples and case studies, both specific and general references that can be combined during the exploration phase of the project in a 'kaleidoscopic' way, thus allowing the origin and emergence of ideas (Young 2003). This apparatus of information, knowledge and experience becomes a fundamental background for the designer since the result of the project action depends on its richness. In this regard, Donald Schön (1993) highlights the difference between the knowledge acquired by a professional in the course of his experiences and that of a student, and how the action then depends on these different backgrounds.

To these repertoires of materials that are used during the creative process also belong the experiences from the disciplinary tradition. The student without direct experience, possessed instead by the professional, can and must humbly refer to what has already been experienced by those who have walked that exploratory path before him, without fear of sinning of poor creativity or being accused of little originality. The importance of experience, understood in this case as a collective experience, is explained by Strawinsky (1942) in some writings in which he deals with the theme of tradition; although referring to a different language, the musical one, they maintain validity and effectiveness also applied to types of composition and graphic representation.

It will be through observation, intended as an instrument of investigation and selection of information, that the raw material necessary for creative and design processes can be acquired. Observation requires a strong curiosity for reality, a necessary solicitation to enrich the archives of knowledge to which the creative and design action appeals in facing that 'kaleidoscopic' combination of images, data, information, elements, from which the design solutions will emerge. It will be the drawing, once again, to serve as a necessary support tool for this process, through the recording of the images that the designers' notebooks and sketchbooks are filled with, which, while often having an autonomous aesthetic value, owe their value mainly to the contribution they are able to make in tackling the most varied and complex design themes. The interpretation of these notebooks clearly shows the relationship between drawing and the observation of reality, the ability to imagine its transformation, its evolution, and consequently the thought of alternative ways of inhabiting the world (Treib 2008). As we will see in the following paragraphs, these ways of working with one's own graphic intelligence are not peculiar to designers, understood in the strict sense, but are transversal to other arts and disciplines.

References

C. Alexander, *Notes on the Synthesis of Form* (Harvard University Press, Cambridge, MA, 1964)

C. Brown, Straight Lines, in *Drawing/Thinking: Confronting in an Electronic Age*, ed. by M. Treib (Routledge, London and New York, 2008)

F. Cervellini, Disegno - la parola - è un patrimonio. in ed. by A. Conte, M. Filippa, Patrimoni e Siti UNESCO: Memoria (Misura e Armonia, Roma, Gangemi, 2013)

R.E. David, Proposal for a diagrammatic language for design. Visible Lang. **1–2** (1972)

C. Dee, Plus and minus: critical drawing for landscape design, in *Drawing/Thinking: Confronting in an Electronic Age*, ed. by M. Treib (Routledge, London and New York, 2008)

H. Gardner, *Frames of Mind: The Theory of Multiple Intelligence* (Basic Books, New York, 1983)

G. Goldschmidt, The dialectics of sketching. Creativity Res. J. (1991)

M.D. Gross, S.M. Ervin, J.A. Anderson, A. Fleischer, Constraints: knowledge, representation in design. Des. Stud. **9**(3) (1988)

D.M. Herbert, Study drawings in architectural design: their properties as a graphic medium. J. Architectural Educ. **41**(2) (1988)

M. Kroeger, *Paul Rand: Conversation with Students* (Princeton Architectural Press, New York, 2008)

P. Laseau, *Graphic Thinking for Architects and Designers* (Van Nostrand Reinholds, New York 1980)

T. Maldonado, *Reale e Virtuale* (Feltrinelli, Milano, 2005)

E. Mari, *Progetto e Passione* (Bollati Boringhieri, Torino, 2003)

E. Mari, *Lezioni di disegno* (Rizzoli, Milano, 2008)

D.A. Schön, *Il professionista riflessivo* (Per una nuova epistemologia della pratica professionale, Edizioni Dedalo, Bari, 1993)

A. Siza, *Scritti sull'architetrura, a cura di A. Angelillo* (Skira, Milano, 1997)

E. Sottsass, *Scritti 1946-2001, a cura di M* (Carbone e B. Radice, Neri Pozza, Vicenza, 2002)

G.N. Stiny, Computing with form and meaning in architecture. J. Archit. Educ. **39**(1) (1985)

I. Strawinsky, *Poetica della musica* (Curci, Milano, 1942)

M. Treib, *Drawing/Thinking: Confronting in an Electronic Age* (Routledge, London and New York, 2008)

J.W. Young, *A Tecnique for Producing Ideas* (McGrawHill, New York, 2003)

Chapter 6
Storytelling with Graphic Intelligence

The previously illustrated relationship between graphic intelligence and design, in the broadest sense of the term, may appear as something peculiar and confined to well-defined disciplinary and professional fields. This aspect should not deceive. Designers are educated to graphically translate their ideas in order to make them visible, communicable and therefore feasible. Analyzing the process of ideation of other types of design, it is clear that in reality it is not a question of disciplinary and design areas but of graphic intelligence. We have seen in the second chapter how, in the field of science, graphic intelligence constitutes an additional tool capable of strengthening one's cognitive abilities. The same can be valid also for the apparently more distant and incompatible fields, such as the field of linguistic intelligence, which tends to be the 'enemy' or at least antagonist of graphic intelligence. And yet this is not the case. Between the two forms of intelligence, the dynamics of fertile collaboration can develop.

In this chapter it is discussed the need to stimulate and to educate the graphic intelligence not only into the education curricula of specific careers, but also in the broader general education, reaffirming the role of graphic representation as communication language for the translation of imagination in images, and for the development of thought in the most different scientific and professional fields and in all the steps of the educative paths. Furthermore, it has been underlined the need to emphasize the autonomy of the graphic intelligence and at the same time the usefulness to strengthen its relations with others kinds of intelligence, so that it will be possible to recuperate the cognitive potential that has been lost, for the restriction of graphic skills to particular professional categories and to few education careers. Therefore, graphic languages have to move from the specialist conception in which they are today confined, towards a broader conception in which they work as tools for the expression, the communication and the thought, not only in the fields of arts, of design and of technic but also—among others—in those scientific and literary.

E. Cicalò, *Graphic Intelligence*, SpringerBriefs in Applied Sciences and Technology, https://doi.org/10.1007/978-3-030-45244-5_6

6.1   Graphic Intelligence in Literature

In educational paths, mainly progressing towards higher education, the graphic intelligence is stimulated and educated only in particular disciplines—such art, design, architecture and engineering—for which graphic languages are considered necessary for the generation and communication of ideas. Instead, the concept of graphic intelligence leads us to rethink the role of graphic skills in relation to broader educational contexts.

Artists and designers, during their training and experience, acquire a *modus operandi* that makes graphic languages and graphic thinking the privileged tools for the production of ideas and for the representation of works and projects on which their professional activity focuses. Their ability to use drawing simultaneously and at the same time alternately to verbal language, their ability to translate mental images into graphic representations, or the naturalness with which they use graphic intelligence to communicate and express thoughts, should be a fundamental objective not only in specialist education but also in generalist education.

However, other apparently distant areas of investigation, like those of science, literature, cinema and theatre, are equally revealing and significant examples of how the graphical intelligence can be an essential tool in many different professional fields. In the field of science, for example, graphic intelligence is an additional tool that can enhance cognitive abilities. The same is true also for other seemingly incompatible fields, such as the linguistic intelligence that tends to be seen as the antagonist of the graphic intelligence.

Indeed, graphic representation can be a powerful tool of thought even in literary fields. Just to read the narration of the way in which Umberto Eco conceived his masterpiece, *The name of the rose*, a novel firstly thought for images and only afterwards for words. In an interview, Umberto Eco claim: 'Everyone thinks the novel was written with the computer, or with the typewriter, actually the first draft was made to pen. But I remember having spent a whole year without writing a line. I was reading, making drawings, diagrams, inventing a world. I have drawn hundreds of labyrinths and abbey plants, basing on other designs, and on places I visited […]. It was a way to get acquainted with the environment I was imagining' (Gnoli et al. 2016). Umberto Eco's words reveal how visual intelligence can benefit from graphic intelligence and again, how these two intelligences are can work together. The first is linked to the ability to process mental images, and the second is linked to the ability to materialize these images so that they can be made visible to others and not only to themselves, and also—perhaps above all—it is linked to the ability to produce images with the eye of the mind through an internal dialogic process similar to that practiced by designers in solving a design problem.

Tolkien's drawings for *The Lord of the Rings* are another example of how the use of graphic intelligence can strengthen the visual intelligence of writers going beyond the concept of illustration, that is to the traditional link between literature. In the first case, an image is a narration-building tool; while in the second, it is a tool for illustrating the narration already defined. Therefore, the relation between these two forms of graphic representation is similar to that between design sketches and design technical drawings.

Graphic intelligence has the power to help solve problems of an ideative kind, whether they are related to the invention of physical or literary works or even, as we will see now, of another kind.

Umberto Eco has described very clearly the importance of drawing in the elaboration of complex literary works in order to better control their narration and make verbal language better adhere to their internal images. Tolkien's drawings for *The Lord of the Rings*, Robert Louis Stevenson's drawings for *Treasure Island*, Jack Kerouak's drawings for *On the road*, J. K. Rowlings for the Harry Potter book series, are some other examples of how the use of graphic intelligence has often enhanced the visual intelligence of writers, going beyond the concept of illustration to which the relationship between literature and image is often traced. In the first case, the image is a tool for constructing the narrative, while in the second it is a tool for visualizing the already defined narrative. We can, therefore, say that between these two forms of representation there is the same relationship already seen, talking about the relationship between graphic intelligence and project, between sketches and technical executive drawing.

6.2 Graphic Intelligence in Cinema and Theatre

Also, the use that film and theatre directors make of this form of drawing, that Mari (2008) defines 'disegno corsivo' is not dissimilar. The studio drawings made by Federico Fellini are perhaps the most well-known. He wrote: 'Why do I design the characters of my movies? Why do I take graphic notes of their faces, noses, moustache, ties, handbags, of how people cross their legs, of people coming to my office? Maybe I have already said it is a way to visualize the movie, to see what kind of film it is, trying to fix something, even tiny, at the limit of the meaninglessness, but that seems to have anything to do with the film, and it is talking to me about it'.

Thus, developing ideas through the use of the graphic intelligence is actually much more usual than what commonly thought. This is clearly demonstrated by the list of film directors as well as, among the best-known, Federico Fellini, Tim Burton, Guillermo del Toro, Pier Paolo Pasolini and Dario Fo. The latter based his speech at the award of the Nobel Prize for Literature in 1997 on those images that allowed him to produce and represent his works. Fo introduces his speech to the King of Sweden in this way: 'The drawings I am showing you have been designed and painted by me [...]. Here, I have been for so long accustomed to making speeches with images, instead of writing them. This allows me to play according to the subject, to improvise, to exercise my imagination and to force you to use your'.

What better example can make people understand the importance of graphic intelligence even for the apparently more distant professions and disciplines than a thank you designed by a Nobel Prize winner for Literature?

6.3   Graphic Intelligence in Media Communication

The success of the new ways of communication stimulates updating the didactic contents of academic curricula in accordance with the new profiles requested by the job market which needs professionals capable of effectively using the new digital media. Nowadays, this effectiveness also depends on the ability to use graphic languages, whose learning thus assumes a renewed centrality. This article discusses the role that these languages play in the educational curricula and in the professional opportunities of degree courses in Communication Sciences.

The degree courses in Communication Sciences are characterized by their generalist approach aimed at offering students the knowledge of a wide repertoire of languages to use, integrate and hybridize within the communication processes.

This particular relationship of complementarity and interdependence between old and new media actually makes it difficult, if not useless, to refer to this hypothetical dichotomy. Old and new media are not to be considered as rigidly separated and alternative categories but as a continuum in constant evolution (Natale 2016). For example, the poster, the most classic and traditional graphic communication product, is now widespread through the web and social networks, in digital format freely downloadable in different formats, sizes and quality, so that it can be printed independently by the public, making possible viral communication campaigns that delineate new ways to vehiculate digital visual communication and to hybridize and contaminate old and new media.

The learning of both verbal and non-verbal languages must now face the new modalities of communication on the new digital media—such as the web, applications for mobile devices, social networks, augmented reality capable of giving new impulses to traditional communication channels and products.

These new modes of communication give graphic languages a new centrality. Indeed, 90% of the information our brain receives is visual. For this reason, visual perception is the most developed and therefore effective and fastest learning channel. Since speed is the characteristic element of the new media of communication, the use of images to convey messages and to catalyze the attention of the audience is exponentially growing. Furthermore, it is estimated that since 2010 mankind has begun to produce every two days a quantity of information content equal to that created since the beginning of civilization. These contents become endless, but attention remains limited and rather it diminishes due to the progressive loss of the concentration capacity connected to the transformation of the ways of the fruition of the new media.

Therefore, today the attention of the public is to be considered more and more as a precious good and the images as an effective tool to earn it (Yacob 2015). Thus, it reinforces the idea of an 'economy of attention' (Davenport and Beck 2001) as a study of the optimal use of scarce resources as is the attention of the audience. In the economy of attention, understanding and forecasting where and how one the observer directs his gaze is the new frontier of research at the centre of the interests of companies that are increasingly willing to make services and applications available free of charge in exchange for the attention of the public that, once collected, becomes goods with a high economic value offered for sale by 'attention merchants' (Wu 2016).

Nevertheless, the whole history and theory of visual communication revolve around this concept of attention. The same word advertising comes from Latin *ad vertere* that means drawing attention to something (Yacob 2015). Giorgy Kepes in *The Language of Vision* also highlighted how the process of visual organization is aimed at defining an area of clarity and intensity in the background of a confused general field that he defines 'the field of attention' and on which the entire Gestaltic theory of form is based (Kepes 2008).

In the Italian educational system, but in the same way in the European one and more in general at international level, the university curricula aimed at training professionals able to codify the graphic languages to gather the attention of the public within the communication processes are mainly of two types: a specialist one—represented by the industrial design courses and in particular of Communication Design, and a generalist one—represented by the courses in Communication Sciences.

In particular, within the degree courses in Communication Sciences of the Italian university, the task of developing graphic and visual skills is entrusted to the disciplines of drawing. However, the contribution of these disciplines is still rather marginal. Of the 42 degree courses[1] currently offered by the various Italian universities, only 5 include ICAR/17 courses, mainly, if not almost totally, held by contract professors. In general, the analysis of the curricula reveals a general weakness in the study of themes related to image and visual communication, often entrusted to the historical-artistic, philosophical, sociological and, only marginally, informatics disciplines. Therefore, these degree courses are mainly oriented towards image analysis and less focused, instead, on their production.

The perspectives for this curriculum are instead linked to the ability to propose professionalizing courses capable of providing the job market with people able to actually produce communication content. The employment opportunities, contrary to the often widespread stereotypes that consider the graduate in communication science difficult to place in the labour market, are encouraging for those degree courses able to follow the transformations of the dynamics of contemporary society and to include in their curricula didactic activities updated in terms of techniques, tools and methods of communication.[2]

Therefore, communication science courses, by their own nature, do not educate specialist skills and are not strictly projectual, but allow students to orient their future career. For this reason, only a maximum of one course is generally dedicated to graphic languages, with the possibility of additional study in the context of degree theses. Consequently, from these reasons, it derives the difficulty in providing all

[1]The degree courses subject to analysis are the three-year courses in Communication Science in Italy, and the data are related to the 2017/18 curricula.

[2]The analysis reported in this article derives from the author's experience as a teacher of an ICAR/17 course called Methods and Techniques of Graphic Representation starting from AA 2014/2015, which over the years has been integrated with the courses of Journalism Languages, Marketing and Advertising Communication.

the basic technical skills in the field of graphic representation and of theoretical-cultural knowledge of visual communication, which instead are generally been in-depth developed in those degree courses that are more focused on these kinds of languages as industrial design courses, totally focused on the use of different visual languages for the projects of communication design.

Since the limits of the lack of technical skills in students' background could discourage a professionalizing teaching approach in graphics classes within humanistic degree courses, their greater awareness of the complexity of communication processes and the greater awareness of communication strategies goes to support approaches that go beyond the traditional theoretical contents focused on the mere reading of the image towards the practice of representation and graphic design. Indeed, the use of visual education often becomes an easy alternative to graphic education, which requires teachers to adopt a more design-oriented approach and a stronger background of technical and professional skills. The problem of replacing graphic education with visual education is actually a recurring problem in all humanistic degree courses, and not only. Instead, visual intelligence and graphic intelligence are confirmed as two different connected but not alternative cognitive areas that should be stimulated, in parallel, in different educational paths and to which the disciplines of drawing can make a fundamental contribution.

References

T.H. Davenport, J.C. Beck, *The Attention Economy: Understanding the New Currency of Business* (Harvard Business Press, Boston, MA, 2001)
A. Gnoli, Umberto Eco: "Così ho dato il nome alla rosa". La Repubblica, 21 Febbraio 2016 (2015)
G. Kepes, *Il linguaggio della visione* (Dedalo, Bari, 2008)
E. Mari, *Lezioni di disegno* (Rizzoli, Milano, 2008)
S. Natale, There are no old media. J. Commun. **66**, 585–603 (2016)
T. Wu, *The Attention Merchants. From the Daily Newspaper to Social Media, How Our Time and Attention is Harvested and Sold* (Atlantic Books, London, 2016)
F. Yacob, *Paid Attention. Innovative Advertising for a Digital World* (Kogan Page, London, 2015)

Chapter 7
Learning by Graphic Intelligence

In this chapter is discussed the relationships between drawing and cognition starting from the concept of graphic intelligence, and going beyond the classic approach, widely deepened in the literature from the field of clinical neuropsychology, linked to a concept of drawing as a tool for the evaluation of the cerebral connections functionalities in cases of particular disabilities. Instead, this article analyzes the relationships between drawing and cognition focusing on learning processes. Therefore, drawing is considered not only as a product with which to interpret the psychological, bodily-kinesthetic and cognitive spheres of the individual but also as a tool for stimulating the development of such spheres.

7.1 Drawing and Cognition

Research on the relationship between drawing and cognition has been largely developed in the field of clinical neuropsychology in order to rehabilitate patients affected by particular forms of neurological disabilities. Within these studies, drawing is generally considered as a tool through which to test the functionality of brain connections (Guérin et al. 1999; Smith 2009). For this reason, these studies generally focus on drawing as a process aimed to graphically reproduce what has been observed, and therefore through which to test the ability to command gestures in a conscious way. Accordingly, in literature, the process of drawing is generally observed and described mainly in relation to the reproduction of what is perceived, with emphasis on the stratification of graphic signs corresponding to the various perceptive phases.

This literature considers Van Sommers's works (1984, 1989) to be the only studies that has really analyzed the relations between drawing and cognition this studies describe two different processes: the first linked to perception and the second linked to graphic production. The first model, linked to the process of perception, is finalized to the re-copying of a subject that is articulated, consistently with the Marr's model (Marr 1982), in three hierarchically structured passages:

© The Author(s), under exclusive license to Springer Nature Switzerland AG 2020
E. Cicalò, *Graphic Intelligence*, SpringerBriefs in Applied Sciences
and Technology, https://doi.org/10.1007/978-3-030-45244-5_7

- a first phase in which the perceived image is represented through a synthetic two-dimensional description based on variations in intensity in which background and figure are not distinct;
- a second phase in which the previous representation is enriched by information about surfaces and placed in a three-dimensional reference system centered on the observer through estimation of distances and orientations;
- a third phase in which, the information relating to the three-dimensionality of the structure of the object represented is completed.

The second model is about graphic production. It consists of four phases. In the act of copying a perceived or a remembered subject, the draughtsman makes a series of choices or decisions (depiction decisions) relating to the characteristics of the drawing. They concern dimensions, orientations, level of detail, etc. Then, the drawing is divided into parts that determine the production strategy. In this regard, two different strategies can be identified: one of hierarchical type, respectful of one form of image organization, and the other independent from it. The identified parts are reproduced according to particular sequences depending on whether the subject is known or not. In the first case, the sequence is defined as a routine program (routine planning), and in the second case it is defined as a contingent planning program, that implies a different approach to representation (problem-solving). Finally, in performing the representation, there can be a series of constraints, both of economic and instrumental nature (articulatory and economic constraints).

From a different point of view, the relationships between drawing and cognition can be analyzed in relation to the ability not to represent but to communicate. Indeed, the development of graphic skills is not different from that of the language skills. Through drawing it is possible to graphically communicate concepts using a particular graphic lexicon and particular syntactical rules that need to be acquired through experience and exercise. Without these, the system of graphic expression remains at a basic level exactly as it happens in subjects not exposed to verbal stimuli during their cognitive development (Cohn 2012).

Therefore, drawing is an activity that produces graphic outputs from inputs of different types: visual, perceptive and mnemonic but also linguistic (Nelson 1996). It must be understood as a system in which the ability to produce graphic outputs is closely linked to the ability to provide inputs (Toomela 2002). For this reason, graphic capabilities cannot be considered as separate from others (Gardner 1983). Indeed, graphic skills have to be considered as a system closely connected to various other skills as motor, imaginative, interpretative, narrative, mnemonic, perceptive, logical, critical and aesthetic skills. Improvements in one of these have an impact on the general capacity of drawing. Thus, the drawing is configured, to the pair of the writing, as a global skill (Hall 2009).

7.2 Graphic Learning: Using Graphic Intelligence

Over time, numerous prejudices have been stratified on the word drawing, which has greatly weakened its meaning and potential. Drawing is traditionally and generally considered an activity linked to a particular individual talent or specific profession. Its real potential as an instrument of knowledge, learning and thought is often ignored. Instead, as the neurosciences explain, drawing allows us to activate different ways of thinking and seeing. When you draw something, you look at it in a different way, focusing your attention on lines, shapes, relationships and details that generally elude to the eye. In our inattentive observation of reality, the brain is satisfied with recognizing what it sees, without deepening the observation, interpretation and understanding of what the eye perceives. Drawing changes the way you look, making active the act of seeing. Indeed, it is a fundamental way of seeing. Milton Glaser explains that when you draw an object, the mind intensely and profoundly concentrates and it is this high level of attention that allows you to grasp things and become fully aware of them (Paivio et al. 1968; Lesgold et al. 1977).

In addition to empowering the ability to understand perceived reality, graphic intelligence improves other learning processes. Based on the learning by doing approach (Wammes et al. 2016), and the traditional use of images as a learning strengthening (Van Meter and Garner 2005; Schwamborn et al. 2010), experiments have demonstrated how drawing can also be an effective memorizing and learning strategy. It has been shown that the drawing of the information to be stored allows achieving better results than other storage techniques because of its ability to enhance the verbal language with the non-verbal language of the images. Words drawn are better memorized than written words, giving rise to what is called the drawing effect (Wammes et al. 2016), which fosters the elaboration of mental images associated with the represented object. The effectiveness of this strategy does not depend on the aesthetic quality of the graphic product; even very fast drawings, realized in a few seconds, allow the achievement of the objective. What counts is not the product but the cognitive process that the realization of that product has succeeded in triggering.

This memorization technique goes beyond the simple association of the image with texts typical of didactic illustration that solicits only visual and perceptive intelligence. By fostering the creation of mental images that can then be translated into graphic representation, drawing stimulates graphic intelligence activating the entire family of spatial intelligence and adding it to the linguistic one traditionally used. Thus, the developed multi-channel cognitive process is clearly more powerful and intense, and it is precisely this intensity of the cognitive strain that allows a stronger rooting of the graphically reworked concepts. Moreover, since drawing implies the control of gesture and movement aimed at the production of representation, the drawing effect would also stimulate kinaesthetic intelligence, further enhancing the cognitive process.

The most recent research in the field of cognitive sciences suggests the existence of important relationships between graphic representation and cognitive development that support the idea of a graphic intelligence independent from the other forms of intelligence that have been until now considered able to describe and contain this particular type of human intellectual competence. Graphical intelligence is the ability to use graphic skills and, more generally, the ability to integrate the use of eye, mind and hand to solve problems of various kinds and generate effective products aimed at creating, acquiring and communicating knowledge.

Therefore, the graphic intelligence should be considered equally important like the best-known linguistic and logical-mathematical intelligence on which the school today tends to focus more. It can complete and enrich the already investigated visual and spatial intelligence that, according to the literature produced so far on the subject, include and coordinate with the skills in the graphic field. Thinking about graphic skills as a form of intelligence obliges us to focus not only on the graphic product but also on the cognitive process that led to the representation of that product. This change of perspective, based on the cognitive potential of drawing, is able to suggest new approaches to didactics at all levels and in all fields of education. Consequently, learning graphics has to be considered preliminary to graphic learning.

In the different phases of cognitive development, the relations between drawing and cognition assume different forms. During childhood it is useful to learn graphic skills in order to enhance the different forms of intelligence that are closely inter-linked. Furthermore, in the following school path graphic skills are useful to enhance the learning of different disciplines. Thus, the transversality of graphic skills emerges, less and less tied to the traditional concept of drawing as a figurative representation of reality and increasingly closer to the idea of drawing as an instrument of thought.

7.3   Learning by Drawing

As neuroscience explains, the drawing activates alternative ways of thinking and seeing. When you draw something you observe it in a different way, focusing your attention on lines, shapes, relationships, details that generally escape your gaze. In our distracted observation of reality, the brain is satisfied to recognize what it sees, without deepening the observation, interpretation and understanding of what the eye perceives. Instead, the drawing changes the way of looking, making the act of seeing active. Drawing is a fundamental way of seeing. Milton Glaser explains that when you draw an object, the mind focuses in an intense and profound way and it is this high level of attention that allows you to grasp things and become fully aware of them (Glaser 2008).

In addition, to enhance the ability to understand perceived reality, graphic intel-ligence enables other learning-related processes to be strengthened. Based on the learning by doing (MacLeod et. al 2010) approach and the traditional use of images for learning enhancement (Paivio et al. 1968), experiments have been carried out to demonstrate how drawing can also be an effective memorization and learning strat-egy. It has been demonstrated that drawing the information to be memorized allows to achieve better results than other memorization techniques precisely because of its ability to enhance verbal language with the non-verbal language of images.

Drawn words are better stored than written words, giving rise to what is called the *drawing effect* (Wammes et al. 2016), which fosters the processing of mental images associated with the represented object. The effectiveness of this strategy does not depend on the aesthetic quality of the graphic product; even very fast drawings, realized in a few seconds, allow the achievement of the objective. What counts, once again, is not the product but the cognitive process that the realization of that product has managed to trigger.

This memorization technique goes beyond the simple association of the image with the texts (Van Meter and Garner 2005; Schwamborn et. al. 2010), typical of didactic illustration, which solicits only visual and perceptive intelligence, because by inducing the creation of mental images that can then be translated into graphic representation also stimulates graphic intelligence, thus involving the entire family of spatial intelligence that is added to the traditionally used linguistic intelligence. The multi-channel cognitive process thus developed is therefore clearly more powerful and intense, and it is precisely this intensity of cognitive stimuli that allows the graphically reworked concepts to take root more strongly. Not only, since drawing implies the control of gesture and movement aimed at the production of representation, the drawing effect would also stimulate kinaesthetic intelligence, further enhancing the cognitive process (Wammes et al. 2016).

References

N. Cohn, Explaining 'I can't draw': Parallels between the structure and development of language and drawing. Hum. Dev. **55**(4), 167–192 (2012)

H. Gardner, *Frames of Mind: The Theory of Multiple Intelligence* (Basic Books, New York, 1983)

M. Glaser, *Drawing Is Thinking* (Overlook Press, New York, 2008)

F. Guérin, B. Ska, S. Belleville, Cognitive processing of drawing abilities. Brain Cogn. **40**, 464–478 (1999)

E. Hall, Mixed messages: the role and value of drawing in early education. Int. J. Early Years Educ. **17**, 179–190 (2009)

A.M. Lesgold, H. De Good, J.R. Levin, Pictures and Young Children's Prose Learning: A Supplementary Report. J. Read. Behav. **9**, 353–360 (1977)

C.M. MacLeod, N. Gopie, K.L. Hourihan, K.R. Neary, J.D. Ozbuko, The production effect: delineation of a phenomenon. J. Exp. Psychol: Learn. Mem. Cogn. (2010)

D. Marr, *Vision* (Freeman, New York, 1982)

K. Nelson, *Language in Cognitive Development* (Cambridge University Press, Cambridge, 1996)

A. Paivio, T.B. Rogers, P.C. Smythe, Why Are Pictures Easier to Recall Than Words? Psychon. Sci. **11**, 137–138 (1968)

A. Schwamborn, R.E. Mayer, H. Thillmann, C. Leopold, D. Leutner, Drawing as a generative activity and drawing as a prognostic activity. J. Educ. Psychol. (2010)

A.D. Smith, On the use of drawing tasks in neuropsychological assessment. Neuropsychology **23**, 231 (2009)

A. Toomela, Drawing as a verbally mediated activity: astudy of relationships between verbal, motor, and visuospatial skills and drawing in children. Int. J. Behav. Dev. **26**, 234–247 (2002)

P. Van Meter, J. Garner, The promise and practice of learner-generated drawing: literature review and synthesis. Educ. Psychol. Rev. **17**, 285–325 (2005)

P. Van Sommers, *Drawing and Cognition: Descriptive and Experimental Studies of Graphic Production Processes* (Cambridge University Press, New York, 1984)

P. Van Sommers, A system for drawing and drawing-related neuropsychology. Cogn. Neuropsychol. **6**, 117–164 (1989)

J.D. Wammes, M.E. Meade, M.A. Fernandes, The drawing effect: evidence for reliable and robust memory benefits in free recall. Q. J. Exp. Psychol. **69**, 1752–1776 (2016)

Chapter 8
Educating Graphic Intelligence

This chapter discusses the concept of graphic intelligence intended as the ability to use graphic skills in order to solve problems and to generate new knowledge in educational curricula. Thinking of drawing as graphic intelligence, supporting the empowerment of the cognitive and imaginative skills beyond the traditional fields of art and design can strengthen the role of drawing in learning paths at each level. Starting from a reflection on the different forms of intelligence involved in the act of drawing, the chapter will discuss the relationship between the improvement of visual and graphic skills and, above all, the importance of developing both within the various formative paths, respecting the differences in terms of meanings, methods and objectives.

8.1 Learning Graphics: Developing Graphic Intelligence

The exploration and the definition of the concept of graphic intelligence force us to focus the attention on drawing as a cognitive process and tool for thinking, so recalling the need to strengthen graphic education within the educational paths. In this way, the graphic education, the drawing teaching, the graphicacy regain their centrality and claim equal dignity as literacy, numeracy and oracy on which school tends to invest more.

Human beings seem to have an innate ability to graphically represent concepts and images, but the achievement of full competence requires that students have to be exposed to a rich graphic environment and has the motivation to acquire fluidity (Cohn 2012). Peripheral skills often come much later in individual development, and can be learned outside of any critical period. In opposition, since drawing requires a limited period of time to be fully activated, this would suggest that it is essential to human cognition like other fundamental functions such as verbal or manual language systems. For these reasons, drawing has to be considered a central rather than peripheral cognitive ability. Therefore, any complete understanding of the mind must incorporate this ability without treating it as an accessory or peripheral system

© The Author(s), under exclusive license to Springer Nature Switzerland AG 2020
E. Cicalò, *Graphic Intelligence*, SpringerBriefs in Applied Sciences
and Technology, https://doi.org/10.1007/978-3-030-45244-5_8

linked only to aesthetic or expressionist intentions. Drawing rather serves as another way to convey concepts, and its study is embedded into the understanding of human communication, human cognition and human nature (Cohn 2012).

The concept of graphic intelligence allows focusing attention on drawing as a cognitive process and tool for thinking, so recalling the need to strengthen graphic education within the educational paths. The graphic education, the drawing teaching, the graphicacy regain their centrality and equal dignity as literacy, numeracy and oracy on which school tends to invest more.

The adequacy of the vocabulary of a language to discuss a particular topic can be significant of the importance of that topic in the culture to which the language belongs. In Italy, the concept of *literacy* is generally used, speaking of initiation of pre-school pupils to the communication languages, only in reference to the education of verbal languages, both in writing and in reading. Although in the other cultures the setting of the children training courses is, in any case, problematic, it is important to observe the richness of the vocabulary available to discuss these topics. The English language, for example, offers the possibility of differentiating literacy in at least four variants: literacy, oracy, numeracy and graphicacy, respectively referring to the education of the written and the spoken word languages, of the numbers, and finally of the graphic signs. They are often defined as 'the four axes' (Balchin and Coleman 1966) in the learning game; but when it comes time to discard one of them, the one you choose is always that of graphicacy, or the ability to communicate through visual messages such as images, maps, diagrams, graphics, symbols and drawings.

Analyzing the educative paths, it is possible to highlight how the verbal languages are more valorized than those non-verbals. Furthermore, in the field of those non-verbal, the perceptive aspects are preferred to those productive leading, in this way, to the weakening of the graphic intelligence. The education of the vision and of the perceptive skills is often considered as similar or alternative to the education of the graphic skills. Consequently, the first tends, for various reasons, to replace the second undermining the possibility to develop one of the most important cognitive tool, that is precisely the graphic thinking. However, learning the languages based on signs, both verbal and non-verbal, concerns not only the decoding processes of the signs perceived but also the complex process of coding of the same signs. So, also the learning of images-based languages requires the development of the coding and decoding the visual information. Therefore, it makes sense to speak of graphic communications to refer to the coding of the message that will be then decoded through the perceptive processes usually associated with the expression of visual communication.

The higher education of teachers is mainly focused on the visual education rather than on the graphic education, with a consequence on the methods they will use in the school classes during their entire career and on the education of generations of pupils and students. These teachers will not have adequate tools to stimulate not only the visual intelligence but also the graphic intelligence too, thereby renouncing the use of these skills to develop and enhance learning. This is also the effect of the lack of adequate teaching and research spaces within the training courses for teachers who will be called to foster the development of these skills in tomorrow's schoolrooms (MacLeod et al. 2010).

Learning graphics and developing the graphic intelligence it is important not only into the education curricula of specific careers, but also in the broader general education, reaffirming the role of graphic representation as communication language for the translation of imagination in images, and for the development of thought in the most different scientific and professional fields and in all the steps of the educative paths. Furthermore, it has been underlined the need to emphasize the autonomy of the graphic intelligence and at the same time the usefulness to strengthen its relations with others kinds of intelligence, so that it will be possible to recuperate the cognitive potential that has been lost, for the restriction of graphic skills to particular professional categories and to few education careers. Therefore, graphic languages have to move from the specialist conception in which they are today confined, towards a broader conception in which they work as tools for the expression, the communication and the thought, not only in the fields of arts, of design and of technic, but also—among others—in those scientific and literary.

8.2 Graphic Intelligence in Curricula

Many preconceptions have been stratified on the word *drawing* over time, which have strongly weakened its meaning and potential. Drawing is traditionally and generally considered an activity linked to a particular talent or specific profession. Its real potential as an instrument of knowledge, learning and thinking are instead often ignored. In the age we are living in, activities related to the graphic sign are in fact generally considered marginal in the evolutionary path of the individual. Useful entertainment during childhood, then an impoverished instrument for the representation of drawing in adolescence and adulthood, the real potential in the more general cognitive development is ignored. As a result, it is not uncommon for students who come out of high school and enter university design courses, where graphic representation must become a language and an instrument of thought, to graphically represent in a way not different from that of children. After the intensity of the stimuli to which they are subjected during childhood, both within the home and school walls, these abilities are in fact less and less stimulated until they are completely forgotten after middle school, with the exception of high school experiences where the graphic sign takes on a purely professional connotation linked to rigidly predefined codes (technical drawing, artistic drawing...).

There is also the paradox that primary school pupils are required to use the same graphic representation models as those required for other higher order schools. Therefore, on the one hand, we have young adults who express themselves graphically as they did during childhood and children who are denied the graphic experimentation inherent to their particular age.

In secondary school, there are two consolidated traditions on drawing didactics: the one with a technical background and the one with an artistic background (Anning 1997). In the design, field drawing is used as a non-verbal language capable of communicating information that verbal language is not able to express. Drawing in this field is distinguished in freehand drawing (exploratory drawing), aimed at representing one's own mental images; technical drawing (representative drawing), aimed at communicating information useful for the realization of the designed artifact. The two graphic modes are closely connected within recursive processes in which the designer dynamically passes from one to the other until the definition and representation of the idea in its final form. Also in the artistic field, the conceptions of drawing can be classified into two types: the conceptual and the representational. Ideative drawing is the one that describes mental images, while representational drawing—so popular in the collective imagination—is aimed at educating the artist in the observation of reality and its faithful translation into image through the coordination between eye and hand.

These are the same models that influence the education of graphic intelligence in kindergarten and primary schools, as discussed above. According to this analysis, the role assigned to drawing in schools has evidently been inadequate since a long time (Cundari 1992). The main functions of drawing are mainly divided into two types: creative and representational (Perry 1992). The spontaneous use of graphic communication in children is closer to exploratory and creative modes than to representational ones. Children, in fact, use drawing to communicate their mental images, where signs are not only able to represent shapes but also abstract elements such as movements, sensations, emotions, sounds, ideas... Their graphic elaborations are closer to the visual translation of a theatrical staging than to the representation of a simple visible form (Anning 1997).

Although there are numerous studies and research on child drawing that have suggested teaching methods useful to guide children's graphic experiences, the attention paid by researchers to the next evolutionary path seems to decrease proportionally with the growing age of the students. This decrease in attention reflects the more general lack of interest in sign and image education that can be recorded in environments where cognitive development takes place, both at family and school level.

Marco Dallari explains that it is accepted the idea that at the end of childhood children stop drawing for 'natural' evolutionary reasons. It is instead evident how culture and education orient and reinforce this phenomenon in the conviction that true knowledge belongs to the sphere of science, rationality, logos and numbers, and drawing and image, belonging to the spontaneous and intuitive dimension of the psyche, belong to childhood and to those few adults (the artists) who for an equally natural gift maintain the spirit and characters of childhood (Dallari 2014).

Anyone who has the opportunity to observe the cognitive development of a child, from the first months of life until pre-school age, can testify that graphic expression is for him an absolutely spontaneous way of communication. Studying carefully their way of communicating graphically, it is possible to observe how this happens naturally, just as it does with verbal language. Their ability to express themselves in a multi-channel way by coordinating eye, hand and brain and then hybridizing this way of communication with other forms such as verbal or kinaesthetic is surprising.

The literature on the subject of child drawing is wide and shows how the process of weakening this way of communication is linked to the strengthening of other ways in which school education tends to invest more. The attention of teachers, and consequently of learners, focuses in particular on the verbal and logical-mathematical sphere, leaving little room for the development of other forms of intelligence. In school age, the expressive and intellectual abilities linked to graphic thought are gradually becoming weaker and homogenized into graphic-visual stereotypes, the origin of which is inadequate training of the teaching staff on the potential of this form of intelligence. As children move from pre-school to primary school, they enter the sphere of writing, reading, numbers and mathematics (King 1978).

Ian Robertson highlights the role of thinking by images in Western society and points out that even this capacity is not sufficiently cultivated in the educational paths, obscured by the enhancement of other intellectual spheres. In fact, Robertson writes that in Western society the word reigns sovereign. At school, the cold web of words envelops the children's minds and it would be disastrous if this did not happen, but everything has a price. By neglecting our imagination we risk withering highly valuable mental abilities (Robertson 2003).

As Angela Anning argues, this passage is also the transition from pre-school literacies (Freire 1971) to primary school literacy, i.e. from a rich variety of 'literacy' (verbal, numerical, graphic, musical, kinaesthetic…) to the prevalence of the literacy of the written words (Anning 1999). She claims that younger children in kindergarten learn by seeing and handling pleasant shapes, and invent their own configurations on paper or clay, thinking through perception. But with the first grade of primary school, the senses begin to lose all educational value. More and more, art is considered an experience in pleasant and fun activities, a sort of mental relaxation. As the studies of words and numbers are more rigorously emphasized, their relationship with art become less intense, and the arts are reduced to one extra, however desirable; ever fewer and fewer are the number of hours per week that can be taken away from the study of those subjects that, in everyone's opinion, have real importance. There are few high schools that insist on giving the arts the time necessary to give some usefulness to the practice of the arts. Even fewer are the institutions in which a commitment to the arts is consciously justified on the basis of an awareness of the fact that they make an indispensable contribution to the development of a rational and imaginative human being. Furthermore, she observes that this educational blurring persists at the university, where the art student is considered an individual pursuing distinct and intellectually inferior skills, although any 'superior' person in one of the most reputable academic areas is encouraged to find a 'healthy recreation' in the art studio during some of his or her free time. The arts in which the student and teacher are trained and graduated do not yet include the creative exercise of eyes and hands as a recognized component of higher education (Arnheim 1974).

However, this condition is not new, but it is the result of a long process that according to Rudolf Arnheim characterizes the entire development of Western culture. In his view, this idea found application and support in the traditional exclusion of the figurative arts from the liberal arts. The liberal arts, so-called because they were the only ones worthy of being practiced by free men, dealt with language and mathematics. Specifically, Grammar, Dialectics and Rhetoric were the arts of language; Arithmetic, Geometry, Astronomy and Music were based on mathematics. Painting and sculpture belonged to the Mechanical Arts, such as to require work and craftsmanship. The high regard for music and the disdain for the figurative arts obviously derived from Plato, who in the Republic had recommended music for the education of heroes, as it involved human beings in the order and harmony of the cosmos, placed beyond the realm of the senses; while the figurative arts, and painting in particular, were to be treated with caution because they reinforced man's dependence on illusory images (Arnheim 1974).

It should not be surprising, therefore, if, at the end of their school career, when they arrive at university, students show some intellectual abilities, or forms of intelligence, which are not very developed and stimulated. Most students start university with a background of experience and skills that have been developed many years before and that, above all, many years before has stopped in its evolution.

As already mentioned, their ability to express themselves and use graphic language is not very different from that of school children. This situation is common to students from all disciplines, both the humanistic, the scientific and design ones. In adulthood, unless one follows an art or design-oriented path, in which these abilities are adequately stimulated through a professional perspective, there is a general renounce to deal with graphic communication. Prejudices, preconceptions, insecurities have over the years become stratified, reducing any possibility of using graphic intelligence to enhance communication and thought not only in the professional and working environment but also in everyday life, thus renouncing a significant part of one's intellectual potential.

Understanding what happens between the starting point and the end of the educational pathways, understanding what is being lost along the way in terms of intellectual potential becomes necessary, even urgent, for those involved in training in the different school orders. The weakening of the graphic-visual and linguistic-expressive spheres is symptomatic and at the same time a consequence of an impoverishment of imagination and curiosity that stimulates to analyze didactic methods, searching for their limits and suggesting alternative approaches. Indeed, the impoverishment of the lexicon, as Faeti (2004) claims, is closely connected with everything that concerns the visual and the image. Knowing how to see is demonstrated with words because every work of interpretation is accomplished only when words are tightened to images that only then exist, because only then are they seen.

Impoverished expressiveness, limited imagery, scarcity of visual experiences and weakness of ideative and project skills appear to be strongly interconnected, where project means not only the project of the exterior world but also the project of the self.

There is a prejudice still strongly rooted in the collective imagination, both in family and school contexts, which leads to approaching the child according to models of limitation. It is the prejudice that leads adults to impose on the child what they think is best for them. The child, as well as the individual of any age, is instead able to benefit from visual, auditive and experiential stimuli of any kind, often much more than adults who are in turn dried up by the imposition of stereotypical models. To focus their attention on stimuli that are presumed to be 'suitable' for them, excluding others that are considered too complex and difficult, impoverishes the potential of their cognitive development, limiting their experiential baggage and evolutive possibilities. In the same way, the imposition of stereotypical graphic codes linked to standardized teaching methods and poor visual imagery precludes an autonomous and peculiar exploration of the self and the world. The poverty of children expressiveness thus achieved will not be dissimilar from the poor expressiveness of these become adults.

Inside and outside the classroom the child is often asked to use the drawing to satisfy the adult's expectations. The subjects of the representations, the symbolic encodings must respond both to the conceptual models of childhood that the adult has absorbed and transmits, and to the visual models that are believed to be appropriate to their age, culture, values, or rather the idea of age, culture and values that the adult cultivates. Thus we are dealing with a sort of schizophrenia between what is the imaginary and the language that belongs to the school sphere and what is developed autonomously by the children first and then by the youngsters (Anning 1999).

The child, at a certain age, ceases to draw because his developmental process is influenced by a culture that has identified thought with the language of words, and has ideologically identified science as the only mature form of knowledge16. As Marco Dallari evidences, in primary school, while the language of words is taught through the learning of its canonical endowments (grammar and syntax), it promotes the widening of the semantic sphere and proposes the listening and reading of authors considered paradigmatic models of good writing. Instead, drawing is proposed either as an accessory apparatus of writing, in a decorative function, or as an instrument of free expression, but in any case, the greater or lesser graphic ability of children is never considered as the result of processes of study, imitation, learning, but as a talent, more or less present, or a natural predisposition (Dallari 2014). Drawing instead represents a fundamental tool for the construction of knowledge and representations of the world. It tends, in part, to seek the representation of objects through criteria of similarity, but at the same time objects are transformed and processed by intelligence as an extension of the relationship that the subject has with the object. Dallari then highlights that the problem of how to educate to the effective use of drawing remains unresolved (Dallari 2014).

In order to understand how graphic intelligence can be educated, it is necessary to start from the knowledge of the state of things that only through direct observation from the inside can reveal its strengths and weaknesses; state of things that in the next card will be represented, in the awareness that the picture we are going to draw represents conditions that are widespread but not generalizable to the totality.

8.3   Graphic Activities in Primary Schools[1]

In this paragraph are presented some reflections developed during teaching workshops held in various schools of different grades, starting from kindergarten and up to middle school. The workshops proposed to promote the development of cognitive thought according to a multi-channel mode that combines the different forms of verbal and non-verbal communication and that, starting from the illustrated book, arrive at graphic representation by concatenating graphic intelligence with visual, perceptive and linguistic intelligence. Visiting the classes as external operators represents a unique opportunity to discreetly observe the world of school from the inside, understand its limits, and at the same time support projects of strengthening and enrichment. This experience, which has been extended over many years to different schools and different educational institutions, has made it possible to observe and record the methods by which graphic intelligence is stimulated and the limits that prevent it from being fully utilized.

The meeting with children and young people in school, from kindergarten to secondary school, is always very intense. The combination of reading aloud with a workshop activity of a graphic type (drawing, painting, collage...) gives particularly interesting results if proposed in a suitable way, by offering stimuli and tools to be re-elaborated in a subjective way, without impositions, but with the declared expectation of a result always appropriate to the request. The proposal combines reading education with visual education through that complex and fascinating tool called the 'illustrated book', a refined object that requires an effort of decoding text and images in parallel (where the image cannot and should not be didactic). Educating the children to listen and look by offering different stimuli at the same time, means asking for high response, sometimes difficult, but always adequate to the great capabilities of his flexible mind.

And yet the best part comes later. After that children have shown good, if not very good, listening and observation skills, the request to express himself through the use of the graphic sign sometimes hesitates to have an equally adequate response to his skills. The older the pupil is, the higher his difficulties will be. The older the children are, the stronger will be their inhibition. Unfortunately, this is an attitude that tends to uniform, full of stereotypes and not capable of experimenting.

Joining classes and proposing workshops based on the Lao Tze philosophy of 'Action without self imposition' so dear to Bruno Munari often finds obstacles. Some didactic principles useful to develop creativity and design thinking such as 'Don't say what to do but how' (Munari) and 'Help me to do it myself' (Montessori) are rarely followed. Sometimes the incompetence of teachers, more often the conditions in which the educator works, leads him to forget and disregard such good practices.

In order to explore the language of graphic signs, shapes and colours and help children to build a personal graphic alphabet, it is necessary to propose the experimentation of materials, tools and techniques. This will lead the pupils to handle tools and methods to be able to express themselves in a personal way, where there is no

---

[1] The authors of this paragraph are Enrico Cicalò and Daniela Melis.

right or wrong result, but the result of an intellectual and creative process. It is easier to activate this process with an audience free of prejudices or crystallized codes, so it is better with children from 3 to 6 years old who are more ready for divergent inter- pretations and productions. Moreover, a good kindergarten school bases much of its teaching on the discovery, manipulation and use of materials and tools as well as on graphic-creative production. It is a fact that most of the time, even in kindergarten, and even more so in primary and secondary school, there are practical 'problems' that undermine the attempt to stimulate the intellectual and creative process.

This happens when the class does not have the most basic materials such as white sheets in A4 format, which in the best of cases are available but are so precious that they can be given sparingly and only one per pupil. In addition to this striking example, there are other questionable requests from teachers who are not used to such practices, such as:

- Maintain the static layout of the classroom by avoiding any noise when moving chairs and desks;
- avoiding the use of materials that dirty the rooms;
- avoid the use of tools that dirty hands or, even worse, aprons (markers, chalk, tempera, etc.);
- prevent confrontation in order to keep silence.

During the workshop activity there are also interferences from teachers related to graphic stereotypes:

- request for correction of graphic design;
- suggestions in order to make the representation as close to reality as possible (even when the children has produced an image representative of an abstract concept);
- solicitations to fill in the blank sheet;
- solicitations to colour better, to use the outline to draw the figures, to colour with spot colours, to use the right colour, etc.

Considering these information deduced from direct experience in various classes of various school grades, it is not surprising that, especially starting from primary school and continuing in secondary school and except in some cases, it can be noticed a psychological block of the children at the beginning of a laboratory experimental path in which it is more difficult to respond to a request for free expression than to punctual deliveries. The question that is most often asked to the operators is 'can I', 'can I do this?', 'can I do it like that?' The answer 'you can do what you want, as you want' always arouses insecurities because it forces the children to find his own way in search of a result that satisfies him and does not respond to explicit requests from the teacher.

After a first estranging impact, fortunately, most children manage to overcome the initial block and can challenge themselves, playing and having fun by finding personal solutions. Some will tend to emulate the others, but it will still be a first step towards experimentation. Seeing what others do and trying to imitate them is not necessarily a bad thing. Often the practitioner also offers working methods to induce people to try. On the other hand, it is by copying others that you learn to do. The 'result' will always be the work of the children who will find his own way of doing, of producing images, of designing, of experimenting not only tools and materials but also his own graphic sign.

Although we can identify better situations in which graphic intelligence has a greater role in enhancing and stimulating graphic intelligence, the previous paragraphs provide a picture of the role of graphic activities in many classrooms. From this overview, some relevant elements can be highlighted:

- the inhibition of pupils to communicate graphically, in comparison to the greater mastery of other communication channels. This inhibition, which not surprisingly increases with the growing age of the pupils;
- the absence of an adequate graphic literacy and methodology in the teaching staff;
- the proposal of graphic and visual stereotypes for the teaching staff; this has to be put in relation with the previous one;
- the perception of graphic activities as chaotic and undisciplined, also in relation to getting dirty with the tools of drawing and graphic representation;
- the inadequacy of investments, including economic investments, which prevent the availability of materials useful for experimentation and the enrichment of graphic intelligence.

With regard to this last point and in relation to what is reported in the previous pages it is useful to remember what John Ruskin wrote in his famous *The Elements of Drawing*, it is not appropriate to engage a child in any practice of art that is not entirely spontaneous. If he has an inclination for drawing, he will fill every piece of paper that comes into his hands with scribbles and he has to be allowed to scribble freely, and he should be duly praised for any sign of his efforts. He should also be allowed, Ruskin writes, to amuse himself with cheap colours as soon as he desires them. He should be lovingly induced by his parents to try to draw in his childish way the things he sees and likes. Parents should praise him but only for the cost of his self-discipline, attention and commitment, otherwise, they will induce him to act for vanity, which is to say always badly (Ruskin 2009).

In addition to the fundamental role of parents and families in the education of this particular form of intelligence—which, like the others today, is often left to the school—the availability of materials to experiment autonomously and spontaneously, the attention to the process and not to the final product are the things that Ruskin also recommended in 1856 for the graphic education of younger children. Exactly what seems to be missing today in many schools.

8.4   Educating the Eye, Educating the Hand

Today's civilization is extremely visual; today's man lives in a world of images that if on the one hand has a practical and utilitarian reason, on the other has its roots in art. This new art is the graphic art that is based on drawing, as graphic compositions are also born on the basis of sketches drawn (De Fiore 1967). Knowing the mechanisms of visual perception, the strategies of the gaze makes it possible to consciously design graphic representation so as to intentionally guide its perception and make visual communication effective. Graphics has evolved without the theoretical reflection that has characterized other disciplinary fields and in a rather fragmented way by investigating particular fields of application more from the point of view of practices than of theoretical and critical reflection (Frascara 1988). The methods, techniques and tools of graphic representation can foster a scientific approach to the processes of encoding and decoding visual messages so that they can both be written effectively and read correctly, really promoting communication between individuals regardless of their origin, culture and identity.

Before starting to use visual language to communicate a message, it is, therefore, necessary to understand how the sensations are created on the level of representation, that is, the space in which the graphic elements selected to communicate the message enter into relation. In order to develop the skills of visual expression, it is necessary to store visual experiences, first learning the basics of visual language and then mastering the graphic representation. One must learn to see as one must learn to speak (Tagliagambe 2005).

Whoever observes something can count on the availability of 'many past experiences' and a considerable amount of 'possible experiences whose result is known in advance' will be able to 'see', in the same situation, many more things than those who do not have them. Above all, it will be able to evaluate an enormously greater number of possible solutions to a problem and to filter into the domain of knowledge only those that are interesting and relevant, choosing the facts and data that best contribute to the solution (Tagliagambe 2005).

Just as to govern verbal language it is necessary to train listening and writing, so to govern graphic language in order to use it in visual communication it is necessary to educate the gaze and exercise graphic expression. The depowering of the graphic-visual sphere is symptomatic—and at the same time it is a consequence—of impoverishment of visual experiences and imaginative abilities. Difficulties of expression, diminished perceptive and imaginative abilities are at the basis of the weakening of creative and planning abilities, where a project is to be understood not only as the project of the external world but also, and above all, the project of the self.

8.5 Visual Education and Graphic Education

Generally, with visual education, or image education, we mean both the understanding and the production of visual images (Bleed 2005) but even in this case, as already seen in Chap. 1, definitions are not always shared (Brumberger 2011) and the production component is always relegated to marginal roles if not completely missing, as shown by the diagram that Avgerinou and Ericson have built on the basis of the analysis of the literature on the subject (Avgerinou and Ericson 1997) (Fig. 8.1).

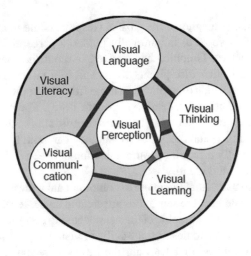

Fig. 8.1 Components of visual literacy (Avgerinou and Pettersson 2011)

The diagram represents the sphere of visual literacy as a family of competences concerning: visual perception, visual communication, visual languages, visual thinking, visual learning. Different are the skills that are included in the literature in the graphic sphere (Delahunty et al. 2012), such as skills in manual drawing, geometry, modelling, spatial thinking, visualization, problem-solving and design. Although there are also in this list some overlapping with the sphere of visual and spatial intelligence. Different nature of graphic education emerges in comparison to the visual education with which it remains strongly connected (Fig. 8.2).

However, it seems that this is not considered in the training system's approach. For example, if we refer to the setting of Italian training it is evident that the two types of education are too often given for interchangeable or equivalent. It is enough to think of the training of teachers who are mainly given visual rather than graphic

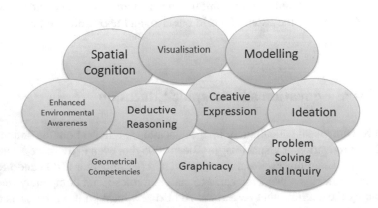

Fig. 8.2 Some core aptitudes associated with graphical education (Delahunty et al. 2012)

training in university courses, with important consequences in the teaching methods they will use in their classrooms throughout their school career and therefore with serious repercussions in the training of generations of pupils and students. It is these teachers who will not have adequate tools to stimulate not only visual intelligence but also graphic intelligence.

Graphic intelligence education today is confronted with some problematic situations including the false belief that graphic intelligence and visual intelligence coincide and the consequent prevalence of visual education over graphic intelligence in high school and university education. What emerges, therefore, is not only the need to rethink the learning path of graphic languages but more generally the concept of didactics and the role of schools in the education of graphic intelligence.

Several studies support the importance of graphicacy, and therefore graphic intelligence, not only in specific professions but also in everyday life to solve problems and deal with situations more generally related to normal social and cultural life. In training courses, on the other hand, more clearly progressing towards higher education, graphic intelligence is only educated to meet the needs of particular disciplines, such as those related to architectural, engineering or industrial design, for which graphic language is considered necessary for the elaboration and communication of ideas.

References

A. Anning, Drawing out ideas: graphicacy and young children. Int. J Technol. Des. Educ. (1997)

A. Anning, Learning to draw and drawing to learn. J Art Des. Educ. (1999)

R. Arnheim, *Il pensiero visivo: la percezione visiva come attività conoscitiva* (Einaudi, Torino, 1974)

M. Avgerinou, J. Ericson, A review of the concept of visual literacy. Brit. J. Educ. Technol. (1997)

M.D. Avgerinou, R. Pettersson, Toward a cohesive theory of visual literacy. J. Vis. Literacy 30(2), 1–19 (2011)

W.G.V. Balchin, A.M. Coleman, Graphicacy should be the fourth ace in the pack. Cartographica: Int J Geogr Inf Geovisualization 3(1), 23–28 (1966)

R. Bleed, Visual literacy in higher education. Educause Learn Initiative Explor 1, 1–11 (2005)

E. Brumberger, Visual literacy and the digital native: an examination of the millennial learner. J Visual Literacy 30(1), 19–46 (2011)

N. Cohn, Explaining 'I can't draw': parallels between the structure and development of language and drawing. Hum. Dev. 55(4), 167–192 (2012)

C. Cundari, L'insegnamento del disegno nelle scuole secondarie superiori. Una ricerca sulla didattica, Disegnare, idee, immagini, 4 (1992)

M. Dallari, Postfazione, in Pizzo Russo L., Il disegno infantile: storia, teoria, pratiche (Aesthetica, Palermo, 2014)

G. De Fiore, *Dizionario del disegno* (La Scuola Editrice, Brescia, 1967)

T. Delahunty, N. Seery, R. Lynch, The growing necessity for graphical competency, in *PATT 26 Conference, Technology Education in the 21st Century*, Linköping University Electronic Press, Stockholm Sweden, 26–30 June 2012, n. 073

A. Faeti, L'erba del cambiamento, in "Hamelin. Note sull'immaginario collettivo", (iv, 10) (Narrare per immagini, Bologna, giugno 2004)

J. Frascara, Graphic design: fine art or social science? Des. Issues 5(1), 1988

P. Freire, *Pedagogy of the opressed* (Seabury Press, 1971)

R. King, *All things bright and beautiful: a sociological study of infants' classrooms* (Wiley, London, 1978)

C.M. MacLeod, N. Gopie, K.L. Hourihan, K.R. Neary, J.D. Ozbuko, The production effect: delineation of a phenomenon. J. Exp. Psychol. Learn. Mem. Cogn. **36**, 671–685 (2010)

L. Perry, in *Towards a Definition of Drawing*, ed. by D. Thstlewood, (Drawing Research and Development, Longman, 1992)

I. Robertson, *The mind's eye* (Random House, London, 2003)

J. Ruskin, *Gli elementi del disegno* (Adelphi, Milano, 2009)

S. Tagliagambe, *Le due vie della percezione e l'epistemologia del progetto* (Franco Angeli, Milano, 2005)

Chapter 9
Conclusions

In the last decades, visual media have become the main form of communication in a contemporary technological society (Bertoline 1998). In the light of this central role that visual communication takes on, it is necessary to rethink graphic-visual skills in the formation of the individual, not only in relation to the exercise of specific professions but more generally in relation to individual intellectual capacity.

The hypothesis, the discussion and the demonstration of a form of autonomous graphic intelligence and its role within the cognitive processes become fundamental to foster a rethinking of the didactics of the graphic sphere today based mainly on the aesthetic-figurative aspects of representation. Rudolf Arnheim, in fact, attributes the weakening of graphic education to the false idea that it is based exclusively on a concept of perception, which is an object of disdain because it is totally separate from thought (Arnheim 1974). Thinking of graphic skills as a form of intelligence forces us to turn our attention not only to the graphic product but also to the cognitive process that led to the elaboration of that product. This change of perspective, based on the cognitive potential of drawing, would be able to suggest new approaches to teaching at all levels and in all fields of education and to strengthen what Arnheim defines as reasoning ability. He claims that educators and educational administrators cannot justify giving art an important position in the educational curriculum unless they understand how the arts are the most powerful means of strengthening the perceptual component, without which productive thinking is impossible in any field of human activity. To neglect art is but the most tangible symbol of the widespread unemployment of the senses in every area of academic study. What is specifically needed is not a more extensive aesthetic teaching or a greater number of esoteric manuals on art education, but a convincing battle in favour of visual thought carried out on an entirely general basis. If we have understood it, in theory, we can try to cure in practice the morbid gap that cripples education and reasoning skills (Arnheim 1974).

What emerges, therefore, is not only the need to rethink the learning path of graphic languages but more generally the concept of didactics and the role of schools in the education of graphic intelligence, which this book wants to investigate.

© The Author(s), under exclusive license to Springer Nature Switzerland AG 2020
E. Cicalò, *Graphic Intelligence*, SpringerBriefs in Applied Sciences
and Technology, https://doi.org/10.1007/978-3-030-45244-5_9

In past years there were substantial increases in the sale of drawing materials1. At first glance, this news may seem a sign of a renewed interest in the graphic arts. However, if we relate this to another equally significant figure, namely the dizzying increase of 1200% compared to the previous year in so-called *colouring books*, which sell 12 million copies in a year in the United States, the scenario changes.

This has been an editorial event that has been able to lift the entire book sector out of the crisis. It is not, however, about the colouring books that we are used to seeing given to children as low-cost, low-commitment entertainment. The audience to which this specific publishing product is addressed is that of adults; adults who are trying to recover their lost confidence with paper and pencil, with that drawing forgotten over the years due to the interruption of stimuli in school and extra-curricular training. The reason for this great interest is to be found in the presumed therapeutic qualities in terms of relaxation and stress reduction attributed, perhaps more for marketing reasons, to repetitive and cognitively non-committal activities such as the sampling with the colours of the predefined and pre-printed contours. No less important in the affirmation of the phenomenon is the sensation that offers their completion to those who colour, that is to say, to have somehow designed and made some graphic product. The fact that this activity practiced by adults in search of cognitive disengagement is actually the same one that is proposed, both inside and outside the school walls, to their children and to all children who instead of cognitive stimuli need it, can only be considered a problem. Science, design and art cannot benefit from the advantages of graphic intelligence if it is not properly educated and stimulated. For this reason, the book closes with a reflection on the role of graphic intelligence in the education of children and in the analysis of the limits and potentialities connected to it.

In exploring the path of graphic intelligence education some problematic situations had been highlighted in this work, such as:

- the prevailing, if not pervasive, focus of school education on literary and logical-mathematical skills, and the almost total underestimation of non-verbal communication channels;
- the false belief that graphic intelligence and visual intelligence are coincident and the consequent prevalence of visual education over graphic education in high school and university education. Visual perception and graphic communication are closely connected but are actually two sides of the same coin. The process of decoding visual messages is fundamental to understand the coding strategies of graphic representation, but coding and decoding messages need to be educated in parallel but also independently;
- the usefulness of stimulating and educating graphic intelligence not only within the training pathways of specific professions but in the broader generalist training, recovering the natural role of graphic representation as a channel of communication useful for the development of thought in the most varied scientific and professional fields and in the different phases of the individual's training;
- the need to highlight the autonomy of graphic intelligence and at the same time the usefulness of strengthening relations with other forms of intelligence so that we can recover the cognitive potential that is largely lost today, relegating it to the

privilege of a few professional categories and therefore of training courses, also through the definition of teaching strategies capable of bringing graphic languages out of a specialized conception to which they are relegated today and bring them back to being useful and often fundamental tools of expression, communication and thought;

- the possibility and usefulness of applying graphic intelligence development models typical of specialist approaches such as design, to other training courses and more generally to all training courses through laboratory practices that give the possibility not so much to entertain but to experiment, practice and appropriate graphic coding methods aimed at enhancing individual cognitive skills and to provide individuals with knowledge and communication tools useful for the development of their personal, not only professional, path.

References

R. Arnheim, *Il pensiero visivo* (La percezione visiva come attività conoscitiva, Einaudi, Torino, 1974)

G.R. Bertoline, Visual science: an emerging discipline. J. Geome. Graph. (1998)

Printed in the United States
By Bookmasters